D1565097

THE FAIR
BUT FRAIL

Nevada Studies in History and Political Science

THE FOLLOWING TITLES ARE AVAILABLE

No. 8
Eleanore Bushnell and Don W. Driggs,
The Nevada Constitution: Origin and Growth
(Sixth Edition) 1984

No. 11
W. Shepperson, N. Ferguson, and F. Hartigan,
Questions from the Past
1973

No. 13
Eric N. Moody,
A Southern Gentleman of Nevada Politics: Vail M. Pittman
1974

No. 14
Ralph J. Roske,
His Own Counsel: The Life and Times of Lyman Trumbull
1979

No. 15
Mary Ellen Glass,
Nevada's Turbulent '50s: Decade of Political and Economic Change
1981

No. 16
Joseph A. Fry,
Henry S. Sanford: Diplomacy and Business in Nineteenth-Century America
1982

No. 17
Jerome E. Edwards,
Pat McCarran: Political Boss of Nevada
1982

No. 18
Russell R. Elliott,
Servant of Power: A Political Biography of Senator William M. Stewart
1983

No. 19
Donald R. Abbe,
Austin and the Reese River Mining District Nevada's Forgotten Frontier
1985

No. 20
Anne B. Howard,
The Long Campaign: A Biography of Anne Martin
1985

No. 21
Sally Zanjani and Guy Louis Rocha,
The Ignoble Conspiracy: Radicalism on Trial in Nevada
Fall 1986

No. 22
James W. Hulse,
Forty Years in the Wilderness: Impressions of Nevada, 1940–1980
Summer 1986

No. 23
Jacqueline Baker Barnhart,
The Fair But Frail: Prostitution in San Francisco, 1849–1900
Summer 1986

No. 24
Marion Merriman and Warren Lerude,
American Commander in Spain: Robert Hale Merriman and the Abraham Lincoln Brigade
1986

The Fair but Frail

Prostitution in San Francisco 1849-1900

Jacqueline Baker Barnhart

UNIVERSITY OF NEVADA PRESS
RENO 1986

Nevada Studies in History and Political Science No. 23

The paper used in this book meets the minimum requirements of American National Standard for Information Sciences–Permanence of Paper for Printed Library Materials, ANSI Z39.48–1984.

University of Nevada Press, Reno, Nevada 89557 USA

Designed by Dave Comstock
Printed in the United States of America

Library of Congress Cataloging-in-Publication Data

Barnhart, Jacqueline Baker, 1940–
The fair but frail.

Based on a thesis (Ph. D.)—University of California, Santa Cruz, 1976.
Bibliography: p.
Includes index.
1. Prostitution—California—San Francisco—History—19th century. 2. San Francisco (Calif.)—Economic conditions. 3. San Francisco (Calif.)—Moral conditions. I. Title.
HQ146.S4B37 1986 306.7'4'0979461 85-28839
ISBN 0-87417-102-4

To
Mike, John, Bob,
and Mom

CONTENTS

PREFACE

Prostitution is seldom found as a designation in labor statistics in the United States. Prostitutes are not thought of in terms of blue-collar workers or white-collar workers. Nevertheless, there have always been descriptive categories within the institution of prostitution, especially in the nineteenth century. As these terms are used in the following chapters, some definitions might be helpful.

Many words have been coined as synonyms for *prostitute,* but in fact *prostitute* is the only word that in the nineteenth century referred to any woman who offered her body for hire or who sold sexual acts for "base gain." No other term, from *whore* to *cyprian,* referred exclusively to prostitutes. For that reason, I use the word *prostitute* to designate all women who sold sex. Other terms describe a specific category of prostitution.[1]

By nineteenth-century usage, *whore* was a coarse term of abuse, almost never used in San Francisco between 1849 and 1851, when prostitutes made up the bulk of the female population. A whore could be a prostitute but could also be a fornicator or an adultress—a woman willing to engage in intercourse with men other than her husband, with or without financial gain. *Harlot* was also a coarse term of abuse and by the nineteenth century referred to women who worked in cheap dance halls or entertained in saloons and prostituted as well.

In England a *doxy* was the prostitute of a rogue. The term was seldom used in the United States except as a synonym for whore. A *cyprian* could be a prostitute or merely a lewd or licentious woman. And a *strumpet* was classed in the same low category as whores, harlots, and doxies.

A *courtesan* (or courtezan), on the other hand, was always a prostitute but only of the highest class. Originally the term referred to a woman of the court or a court mistress; it remained a prestigious description and was never used as a term of abuse. Courtesans were often kept by one man at a time, but usually without any pretense of love or permanency. A *mistress* or *paramour,* however, was the illicit ladylove of a married man. The mistress was a prostitute only if her motives were known to be financial. It is the only term dealing with illicit sex that includes the word *love* in the definition.

Beyond the classifications of working prostitutes were bawds and madams. *Madams* ran the elite parlor houses and better-class brothels. *Bawds* supervised the functions of cheaper brothels and houses of prostitution. Such women were often too old to prostitute any longer (that is, were unable to attract customers). Some had managed to save sufficient money to open houses of their own. Others had executive abilities that the nineteenth century did not give them the opportunity to put to other use. (Before 1700, bawds were men employed to procure girls for kings and other members of the royal courts. After 1700 the word designated a woman who was employed in pandering to sexual debauchery, a procurer, or a keeper of a place of prostitution. As a male occupation, bawdry was respectable; as a female occupation it was deprecated.[2])

A variety of terms also were used for the places of prostitution. *Brothel,* of course, designated any house of prostitution. A *parlor house,* though, was the elite location where graciousness and decorum were maintained. A *crib* was the most degraded kind of house. It was usually built exclusively for prostitution and consisted of numerous small (six-by-eight-foot) rooms all opening onto the street by door or window, allowing the prostitute to attract customers. *Bagnio* (originally an Italian bath house) and *bordello* were used as synonyms for brothel.

All of the terms defined above have little meaning in today's world of prostitution, and in the nineteenth century they were often casually interchanged without concern for their definitions. Nevertheless, they were descriptive of the various categories of prostitution and were used as such by those who wrote specifically about the institution. Other terms that I use are explained in the text, but my use of the word *professional prostitute* needs additional clarification.

In the 1860s the term *professional* applied to anyone (virtually always male) who was good at his job and knowledgeable about it and who had raised his trade to a dignified status. I would add that professionals maintain standards set by themselves or by their trade. By both these definitions, many nineteenth-century prostitutes could be called professional and probably viewed themselves as working women rather than as deviants or victims.

For the prostitutes who migrated to San Francisco in the first few years of the gold rush, there was very little competition to test their compliance with the criteria of professionalism. Many took their profession a step higher and became entrepreneurs, willing to risk their lucrative jobs working for others in order to open businesses of their own.

Entrepreneurship was almost a mania in San Francisco during the gold rush. Women's opportunities in prostitution paralleled men's opportunities in other frontier occupations, and, like the men, many tried to go into business for themselves, giving up prostitution to become madams or to buy and run gambling saloons or barrooms. Some had been prostitutes in other places and had migrated to San Francisco for financial rewards. Others became prostitutes because of unexpected financial need. For a woman who had to support herself and her family, the options for employment were limited. One choice that she had was prostitution.

No matter how solitary the act of writing, no book is prepared without help. My list of thanks seems endless: students, friends, and casual acquaintances who raised questions and offered an outlet to test ideas; my family, especially my three sons, who pushed when necessary and were supportive at all times; colleagues who were willing to give up their time to read and comment on various stages of the manuscript.

I would like specifically to thank professors Judith Stanley, John Dizekis, and David Sweet for their invaluable help with the manuscript in its original form. The revisions probably wouldn't have been completed without the chapter-by-chapter critique of professors Joanna Cowden, Don Lillibridge, Kirk Monfort, and Dale Steiner. Librarians are invaluable to any scholar, but the librarians at the Bancroft are unsurpassed. And finally, my endless thanks to Nancy Riley for her expert typing and incredible memory.

I. INTRODUCTION: A WOMAN'S PLACE

A study of prostitution and its relationship to the larger society reveals that the institution always reflects prevailing social attitudes and that prostitutes—like businesspeople everywhere—respond to consumer demand.

This social pattern is evident in San Francisco during the period from the gold rush to the end of brothel prostitution. During the 1850s, 1860s, and 1870s in San Francisco, prostitutes were first admired, then tolerated, and finally ostracised (in public) by the general population.

The frontier was a male society, and the percentage of females present was small. Therefore, in the early years in San Francisco, the scarcity of women served to increase the appreciation of the few who were there. What a woman was did not matter so much as the fact that she was a woman. Prostitutes were not viewed as deviants from the norm, because there was no norm. As a result, prostitutes did not attempt to hide their occupation, and society used such polite euphemisms as "the fair but frail" to describe them.

By the late 1860s, when a modified Victorian culture had begun to exert some influence in San Francisco, prostitutes were forced to retreat in visibility, although condemnation was reserved for the harlot and whore (coarse terms of abuse, meaning women who engaged in illicit sex). By the late 1870s and 1880s, when, under the influence of the Victorians, social restraints were employed to regulate morality, men who had responsible reputations to uphold in society were governed by the rules. To be seen with a noted prostitute was to break one tenet of the basic code of the culture: public respectability.

By the late 1870s, the city was no longer characterized by the entrepreneurial gambler, speculator, and "businesswoman." Frantic attempts to make a fortune at any scheme became fewer as competition increased; prostitutes who, by their very scarcity, had been the objects of competition by potential customers in the 1850s were now the competitors. This basic premise of capitalism—supply and demand—was a further factor in the changing world of prostitution in San Francisco.

Those professional prostitutes who began arriving in California in the spring of 1849 were as much a part of the gold rush as the miners. But like the gamblers and speculators, they recognized that the real profits were to be made in San Francisco, where the miners came to spend their money.

At this time, the market clearly favored the prostitute. The ability of professional women to take advantage of these unique opportunities determined both their financial success and their social freedom. They were working women, often self-employed, and in great demand in a society temporarily free of condemnation of them. The political, economic, and social conditions of the world in which they worked affected their public acceptance—and their self-image—in the same way such conditions have affected prostitutes from the days of the Sumerians to the present.

Despite being the world's oldest profession, prostitution has a peculiar historical ambiguity. Everyone knows what prostitution is, no one denies its existence, but societies from the time of the Sumerians (c. 2000 B.C., the first recorded reference to prostitution) to the present have never been able to decide if prostitution is good or evil, natural or deviant, a crime, a sin, or a necessary service. Whenever the social evaluation of prostitution changed, it was not because the profession changed but because society chose to define it in a new way.

In the Sumerian–Babylonian *Gilgamesh Epic,* the temple prostitute was praised as the teacher of "morals and manners," and she and her contemporaries were free to marry. A short time later, attitudes changed and fathers began to instruct their sons "not to marry prostitutes" because they would not be loyal and supportive.[1]

In ancient Greece, prostitution flourished. There were even state-owned brothels whose purpose it was to make "Athens an attractive city." But in the utopias of Plato and other Greek philosophers, prostitution was to be eliminated completely, although, to "promote good feeling among men," women and children were to be shared.[2]

In other places in the ancient world, prostitution was often viewed as sacred—and therefore not a disgrace. When the "handsomest girls" in Dahomey were trained as "public harlots" by prostituting themselves to priests and seminarians, society believed them to be "married to the god" and directed in their "excesses" by him. In Babylon, Syria, and Cyprus, women were "obliged by custom to prostitute themselves to strangers at the sanctuary of the goddess."[3] But in the changing social order under Constantine (c. 300 A.D.) such "sanctified harlotry" was abolished along with the "temples of prostitution." The new monotheistic Christianity, which in its earliest stages was a male-oriented religion, attempted to end the worship of mother goddesses, sex, and sexuality.[4]

Even when a society condemned prostitution, the action was often equivocal. Moses is said to have tried to eradicate prostitution among the Jews and yet "connived at the intercourse" of young Jewish men with "foreign prostitutes." As long as the women were not Jewesses they were allowed to practice their trade in tents along the major highways, and lawmakers viewed their activities tolerantly. In the same vein, biblical references to Judah and his daughter-in-law, Tamar, reveal a contemporary tolerance for prostitution as long as the prostitutes were professionals. When Judah mistakes Tamar for a prostitute and makes her pregnant, he has her burned for having "played the harlot."[5]

In such societies, prostitution was acceptable provided class lines were maintained. In the regime of Charlemagne, the elite of the profession were kept by the rich in *gynecea* (women's rooms), while the common prostitutes were "to be scourged and a like penalty" inflicted on those who kept "houses of debauch." What was a crime for the poor was established custom for the rich, encouraged and sanctioned by law and by the church.[6]

Later attempts by kings, churches, and legislators to regulate sexual practices varied according to the times. In the thirteenth century, the French kings Louis VIII and Louis IX attempted the "total extirpation of sexual vice" by expelling prostitutes "across the border." Catherine de Medici (c. 1550), on the other hand, is said to have used prostitutes to learn the secrets of "politicians of the day" and thereby secure her position in the French court. An English parliament under Henry II seemed determined to organize, not outlaw, the bagnios or stews by ordaining, among other things, that "No single woman [was] to take money to lie with any man [in the brothel], but she lie with him all night till the morrow."[7] In the eighteenth century, France was still attempting to regulate or end prostitution. One method used was to forbid women to walk the streets in any way that would attract customers. The undaunted prostitutes "advertised their charms by appearing stark naked at their windows."[8]

Prostitutes are adaptable; they have to be, since their legal, moral, and social position is determined by society's view of women in general and women's sexuality. At one point in time or in one civilization, a woman's worth might be measured by the success or failure of her husband, or by her ability to serve or encourage men to greatness, or by her ability to produce children.

By the fifth century A.D., Christians concluded that the Second Coming of Christ might be delayed, and in order to perpetuate the faith, the Constantinian denigration of women had to be reversed. Matrimony became a sacrament, not a contract; fidelity to one's spouse became a rigid standard. While the prostitute was only a sexual creature, the "honest" woman became a mother, subordinate to men but gaining dignity and respect. By sanctifying motherhood and by decreeing intercourse a means of procreation only, not of pleasure, society placed women on an asexual pedestal.[9]

When the situation was reversed, and women were admired for their sexuality, they often became the victims of sexual freedom. One of the most graphic examples of such a juxtaposition was in the Humanist era of the sixteenth century, which was itself a reaction to the power and control of the Christian church over society. As in the early Christian era, this was a male-oriented movement but with a renewed interest in the sensuality of women. Lorenzo Valla asserted "that prostitutes were far more useful than nuns and that the highest social ideals enjoined female promiscuity."[10] Female promiscuity, in this instance, was to enable the great male thinkers of the day the opportunity to relax after their labors. During the Renaissance, history recorded many women of note, but those most notable were courtesans and mistresses.

Although prostitution in the western world had become a business in all essential elements by the eighteenth century, societal attitudes toward women helped to structure the business. It was organized primarily into brothels with a managerial class: madams, bawds, and procurers. There was a hierarchy within the profession, from the common streetwalker to the courtesan, and there was competition among the better-class brothel keepers to attract customers. Such competition might take the form of adding elements of grace and charm to the brothel with luxurious furnishings, musical entertainment, and elegant suppers. Others might cater to the more recherché demands of their customers. What did not change was the constantly fluctuating attitude of society based principally on the prevailing attitude toward women's sexuality.

The "honest" women of England were lauded by their countrymen as "chaste, delicate and virtuous," unlike the "strumpets" who filled the brothels of London. In France during the same period, professional prostitution was seldom condemned. The "general desire to intrigue" was fashionable, and in France "not to be fashionable [was] a condition much more dreaded than not to be virtuous."[11]

Both countries, however, in the seventeenth and eighteenth centuries, sought methods of ridding themselves of the least desirable members of the trade. One solution, perhaps as much to the advantage of the women as to the mother country, was to send convicted prostitutes to the colonies.

Many of these women were thus able to increase their options, marrying and raising families in the New World.[12]

In the New World colonies, prostitution in its most common form was slow to develop. In the first place, women were scarce and usually had the option of marriage over prostitution as a means of economic survival. Secondly, many of the New England colonies were founded as potential Christian religious utopias, and prostitution was not countenanced. In addition, development of the plantation system in the southern colonies, with its supply of slaves, made prostitution less likely to develop there. As Howard B. Woolston concluded in his history of prostitution:

> *A [slave] woman whose body is the actual property of a man, in the same way as is that of a horse or a cow, to be disposed of as he sees fit, finds any physical attractiveness she may possess a distinct ban to virtue. In a society which accepts as a matter of course a double standard of sex morality and a belief in the physical necessity of the sex act for men, it is to be expected that the presence in its midst of a group of women without legal right to their own persons would make prostitution in its accepted sense almost unnecessary.*[13]

But as the colonial population expanded, as more and more "undesirables" from the London slums were transported to the New World, the officials began to face the problems of "licentiousness." In 1676, a Maryland rector wrote, "All notorious vices are committed; so that it [the colony] is become a Sodom of uncleanness and a pest-house of iniquity." No doubt the rector was overreacting, but even in the Puritan colonies enough laws and ordinances were being passed against "fornication, keeping of bawdy houses, night walking, and adultery" to indicate that the Old World vices the Puritans had hoped to escape still existed.[14]

When the colonies of the Old World became the first republic of the New World, a commitment to democracy included a change in attitude toward prostitution. No longer were there special social, legal, or moral laws for the elite of society. In a world where all men were to be equal, all "fallen" women were equally guilty. Brothel prostitution became linked with vice and crime. Consequently, by viewing prostitution as part of a subculture, society was able to explain it away as deviant female behavior and, to a degree, to ignore it.

In fact, American prostitution has never been an isolated subculture. It has always been firmly integrated economically within the community. Politically, it has always affected legislation and the enforcement of various laws and ordinances. For the most part, however, the interaction between prostitution and the political and economic activities of society was covert. Prostitution was never openly acknowledged, because that would offend the moral sensibilities of the larger society. This situation was especially evident during the second half of the nineteenth century, when what is often referred to as a "Victorian" culture exerted the most influence on American society.

Anthropologist Clifford Geertz has given us a definition of culture that is probably more relevant to Victorian values than to any other. "Believing, with Max Weber, that man is an animal suspended in webs of significance he himself has spun, I take culture to be those webs, and the analysis of it . . . an interpretive one in search of meaning."[15] Culture, Geertz goes on to explain, "is public." We choose from our past that which most clearly reveals what we wish our image to portray. But as the web is of our own weaving, it changes to fit our present ideals and future goals.

In the nineteenth century, the ideals and goals of Americans allied them more closely to the British than any other national identity. Because of language, history, and economic interdependence, the cultural connection between the two countries was strong and, in part, explains why a certain segment in both societies (between approximately the 1840s and 1900) shared a culture that has been labeled *Victorian.* The fact that Americans accepted the use of Queen Victoria's name to identify a culture and, indeed, an era in their own social history was clear evidence of the close relationship between the two countries.

The Victorian culture had a value system emphasizing public images and actions. The writings of the Victorians were prescriptive. Victorians were interested not only in defining the values of their culture for themselves, but in shaping the quality of life for others. Stressing social responsibility and personal morality, they hoped to humanize the new industrial capitalism of the Civil War and post-Civil War period. By placing a high priority on a "rational order" for themselves as well as for society, they were confident that both objectives could be accomplished.[16]

While American Victorians were not the majority of the population, they were the most vocal; through their control of the literature of the time, they heavily influenced public opinion. Victorians in both Britain and the United States were members and supporters of the class that controlled the economic institutions of their countries. But, whereas in Britain this middle class had to struggle against an aristocratic culture for political and social influence, in America the middle class—the Victorians—dominated the social and political as well as the economic institutions.[17]

The spokesmen for the Victorian culture were primarily urban northerners: conservative, literary, and active participants in the expanding industrial world. Since they controlled the media of the day—the newspapers, magazines, fiction—their intellectual and social influence was extensive. Fully committed to their goals, they took themselves and their views of virtue, duty, and morality so seriously that they became dogmatic. Their method of instruction through prescriptive literature was so heavily weighted with moral messages that it did not reflect reality. The supposed *natural* absence of sexuality in women was only one such example. The critics of the Victorians have labeled them hypocrites because of their inconsistencies. This attitude is unfortunate, because it ignores the essence of the culture: public conformity. The Victorians, "suspended in a web of their own weaving," continued to reinforce prescriptive morality because sexuality or sexual drive presented the wrong image of what they recorded as the true essence of their culture.[18]

The most influential period of Victorianism was between 1850 and 1870; as its influence began to diminish, however, defenders of the culture grew even more rigid in their beliefs and were increasingly determined to institutionalize their fundamental values. Morality, duty, and the quality of life were no longer left to individuals to strive for; society became the responsible institution.

By the last twenty-five years of the century, social work

(for example, in the form of rescue missions, orphanages, and, in the 1890s, settlement houses) began to be carried on by secular groups rather than by churches. Librarians of the 1880s attempted to censor popular "fiction that offended genteel sensibilities." The books they found objectionable were written for women, and a common trait amoung them was the rejection of traditional authority: religion, the home, and the dominant male.[19]

Acceptable Victorian literature did not err in its moral message. Although such material was not limited to women's themes, women were the largest group of readers, and the bulk of material was therefore directed toward them. This fact was perhaps both the cause and the result of the Victorian determination to preserve and sanctify the home, conceived as the undisputed domain of women and as the arena for their fullest self-expression. A rational ordering of life was the goal, and as women controlled the earliest training of children it was therefore important that they perpetuate the ideals and values of Victorianism through their children. Developing a consensus on childrearing was something that could not be left to chance.

Subtlety was not a feature of Victorian didactics, yet Victorian methods of instruction satisfied the needs of a rising middle class that wished to learn how to behave "properly." As a result, during the last half of the nineteenth century, etiquette and advice books were published almost by the linear foot. Instructions, rules, and practical information were offered for every conceivable social situation, from eating with a knife—a fork was reportedly less dangerous—to the proper method of borrowing mourning attire for a funeral.[20]

Etiquette books gave instructions on how to raise children, dress, set a table, write letters, walk, talk, greet your husband (mother, sister, friend), show the proper emotion for given occasions, greet royalty or servants, smell flowers, laugh, eat, faint to prove one's delicacy (including a list of items that should make a proper lady faint), and on and on without apparent end. Victorian women were to portray the culture's successful model; therefore their public image was to be flawless. Any deviation from the role of "lady" was a sign of weakness or vulgarity. Victorian men were not ignored in the prescriptive literature, but the majority of the advice was directed toward women.[21]

Moral weakness was to be avoided at all costs. By striving to conform to the image described in literature, one would not only reach the desired personal goal but would be an example to the rest of society as well. This feature of Victorianism is enough to alone explain the Victorian attitude toward prostitution, the antithesis of all "important" institutions of authority: legal, moral, and social. Thus prostitutes were the antithesis of the proper woman, who in the 1850s and 1860s was pure, pious, gentle, naive, delicate, and fragile. By the 1880s she was still all of these things but not quite so naive. Though physical love became an acceptable emotion, it was not to be confused with sexuality, sensuousness, or sexual drive.

It is in the area of sexuality and sexual drive that one confronts the greatest contrast between Victorian ideals and fact. While Victorian moralists preached asexual ideals, red-light districts flourished. One might argue that the prevalence of "sex for hire" was indicative of sexual repression between husbands and wives. Since customers in brothels were men, many of them married, it seems reasonable to assume that the men were being sexually frustrated at home and had to satisfy their sex drive with prostitutes. But this explanation is too simplistic and at the same time too complicated.

Such a view of Victorians can be found in the writings of William Acton, a nineteenth-century British physician who did extensive studies of prostitution and sexuality in England. He claimed that proper women had little or no sex drive, and that those who did were not normal. "I should say that the majority of women (happily for them) are not much troubled with sexual feelings of any kind." If Acton were correct, the argument stands: if proper, normal Victorian wives, with no sexual feelings, submitted to their husbands only out of duty, then the proper Victorian husbands, not wishing to cause their wives unhappiness, would understandably seek sexual relief at brothels—with women who were "not normal."[22]

Acton's sexual-advice books were widely read in the United States as well as in England. There were also many other medical men in both countries who endorsed Acton's theories, and the theories reinforced the Victorian image of proper womanhood. But the question remains whether the theory was based on what women actually felt or on what medical men like Acton thought they should feel. Among the popular and scientific medical literature of the period (approximately 1850–1900) there was divided opinion on the question of female sexuality.[23]

Books on sex by doctors Charles Taylor (1882), Orson Fowler (1870), and George Napheys (1869) are examples of popular medical literature opposed to Acton's views. Taylor warned women of the danger to their health in denying their sexuality. Fowler claimed: "That female passion exists, is as obvious as that the sun shines." And Napheys, though recognizing the existence of women without "sexual feelings," listed them as the smallest of three classes. A larger group were women with "strong passion," and the majority were women with a moderate "sexual appetite." A fourth writer in Carl Degler's list, Dr. Ely Van de Warker (1878), went even farther, claiming that the absence of sexual feeling in women was as abnormal as impotency in men and just as "worthy of medical attention."[24]

The doctors quoted in Degler's article were writing on medical subjects other than sexuality and the sex drive in women. Their material merely assumed the existence of sexuality, which is important indirect evidence of its existence. As Degler observes, however, setting up one group of writers against another proves nothing except that opposing views existed. However, Degler offers supporting evidence in the form of a survey on the sexuality of middle-class women who were raised during the Victorian era.[25] Although the number of women interviewed was small, the survey shows that a majority of the women polled felt sexual desire and experienced orgasm. Most of the women were equally adamant that the purpose of sex was pleasure and fulfillment of a natural appetite. Most importantly, the women considered their sexual desires and reactions normal and natural.[26] How do we reconcile these conclusions with the commonly accepted view that the Victorians were sexually repressed?

The first step is to dispense with the term "sexual repression". The Victorians did not use such terminology. As

Degler notes, "the excessive gentility of the middle class has been read by historians as a sign of hostility toward sexuality, particularly in women."[27] Those who have drawn their conclusions from the combination of excessive gentility and the views of men like Acton have a distorted image of the Victorians. That the etiquette and decorum books of the period were prescriptive rather than descriptive is seldom questioned. Why, then, should there be any surprise that sexual advice was also prescriptive, designed to transform a very different reality? To improve themselves, the Victorians had to fight the "bad passions" within themselves. But no one suggested that intercourse between husband and wife was a bad passion. On the contrary, the Victorians encouraged families. In fiction, love plus marriage produced perfect children, while seduction or loose morals produced weak infants who usually died. The message was quite clear, and it had nothing to do with the avoidance of "proper" sexual behavior.

There is no doubt that Acton (and his American following) told women how they should behave sexually. Was this, however, the important message he wished to convey? Women were dealt with only twice in Acton's book *Functions and Disorders.* When he claimed that women were not troubled with "sexual feelings of any kind," he added:

> *As a general rule, a modest woman seldom desires any sexual gratification for herself. She submits to her husband, but only to please him.*[28]

In an earlier reference to women, Acton assures men:

> *It is a delusion under which many a previously incontinent man suffers, to suppose that in newly married life he will be required to treat his wife as he used to treat his mistresses. It is not so in the case of any modest English woman. He need not fear that his wife will require the excitement, or in any respect initiate the ways of a courtezan.*[29]

Acton's claim that middle-class wives had little or no sexual drive was meant to reassure men, not to dictate to women. In order to improve public morals, he urged men not to spend time with prostitutes and courtesans. One of the causes he gives for disorders of the reproductive organs is excessive sexual activity, which is, he warns, debilitating. The cure was to give up the prostitutes and courtesans who made excessive sexual demands and, instead, choose a wife who (he assured) would not "require the excitement . . . of a courtezan"; would "submit . . . but only to please"; and would give no cause to suffer.[30]

It is interesting to note that Acton, the most widely quoted "expert" on the absence of sexual desire or needs in women, placed all sexual responsibility upon them. If they were sexual, that is, prostitutes or courtesans, they led men to ruin by excessive demands. If they lacked sexuality—as proper wives did—they saved men from themselves.

The same year that *Functions* was published (1857), another book by Acton, *Prostitution,* was also. In his study of prostitutes, Acton did not deny sexuality to women. "What is a prostitute? She is a woman who gives for money that which she ought to give only for love. . . ."[31] The sexual drive in prostitutes was not only misdirected, it was so excessive that it caused debilitation and ill health in the unsuspecting men who fell prey to it.

In his work on prostitution, Acton showed a more open or realistic attitude than his general view of women would suggest. He advocated, for example, the regulation and licensing of prostitutes, something which most Victorians refused to consider.[32] To the arbiters of society, regulating prostitution would require public acknowledgment of its existence—would, in effect, legitimize prostitution, contradicting the culture's function, which was to portray Victorian values publicly.

The attitude revealed in the two works by Acton would appear, on the surface, to be inconsistent, but not if the goal of Victorian literature is kept in mind. The Victorians did not report, they advised; they did not describe, they prescribed. Acton the doctor wanted prostitution regulated to stop the spread of disease; Acton the Victorian chose the most effective method to convince his readers that prostitutes were the pitiable victims of social disorders that only society could change. The goals of *Functions* were different and called for other methods. Acton advocated controlling the "bad passions"; patronizing prostitutes was clearly giving in to a bad passion.

Events in the world of prostitution in the last half of the nineteenth century suggest the Victorians were not very successful. It was a period of the most blatant prostitution ever witnessed in the United States. Every city had its notorious red-light district. Street-preaching moralists were daily predicting heavenly retribution against the Sodom and Gomorrah areas. In one sense, the red-light districts can be viewed as enclaves of defiance against uncompromising middle-class codes, which attempted to dictate morality to all classes while reinforcing class distinctions. The continuation of such notorious districts as the New Orleans French Quarter, Denver's Street of Red Lights, or San Francisco's Barbary Coast supports the idea that "the social history of their own sexual experiences was not part of the Victorians' official consciousness of themselves or their society."[33] When they mentioned prostitution, it was to condemn it, but they seldom used their influence to force police and legislators to put an end to it. By the early 1900s, a new generation of progressive leadership, one with less faith in the success of "public example," demanded and got enforcement of vice laws and ordinances. By 1910, red-light districts were disappearing across the nation and would continue to decline as red-light abatement laws were passed from 1914 through 1924. Prostitution, of course, did not disappear but entered a new era, which reflected new attitudes about women, their role, and their sexuality.

II. "THE TIME WAS THE BEST EVER MADE"

Enlargement of Society—We are pleased to notice by the arrivals from sea Saturday, the appearance of some fifty or sixty of the fairer sex in full bloom. They are from all quarters—some from Yankee-land, others from John Bull country, and quite a constellation from merry France. One Frenchman brings twenty—all they say beautiful! The bay was dotted by flotillas of young men, on the announcement of this extraordinary importation.

ALTA CALIFORNIA, *May 7, 1850*

The "fairer sex in full bloom" was an *Alta* euphemism for prostitute, and both the announcement and the "flotillas of young men" sailing out to meet the ship were indicative of the continued shortage of women in gold-rush San Francisco. The ratio of men to women in 1849 averaged fifty to one, and as long as that shortage of women continued neither the *Alta* nor the populace would condemn the arrival of fifty or sixty women, even if they were prostitutes. The *Alta* did not follow up its story of May 7, but it can be assumed that the women were professionals and moved into the professional hierarchy in San Francisco, just as did the seven hundred or so who had arrived the year before.

The development of the institution of prostitution on the frontier began in the same entrepreneurial spirit that was characteristic of so many aspects of early San Francisco society. By definition, to be an entrepreneur one had to work on one's own to amass a fortune, accepting the risks for the sake of the profit. It was an unusual place and time; what back home had been merely an occupation here became a profession, a way to speculate in the new land of unlimited opportunity. As Eliza Farnham, an early settler in California, observed; if a man "could blow a fife on training days" in the East, "he could be a professor of music here."[1] And if a woman had been a harlot in New York, New Orleans, Paris, or London, she could immediately become a courtesan in gold-rush San Francisco. The opportunities for upward mobility among professional prostitutes were remarkably similar to those that the men enjoyed in other professions. There was no traditional merchant class to close ranks against a newcomer—everyone was a newcomer; there was no professional organization from which an outsider had to gain acceptance; and there was no organized red-light district to check competition among the "fair but frail."

The immigrants to California represented nearly every occupation, every race, and every nationality on the globe. But there was a similarity among the gold seekers that "tended to give a peculiar character to the aspect of the place and habits of the people," and this was that by and large they were adult males under forty years of age. Among the forty-thousand immigrants who arrived by ship in 1849, a woman, child, or elderly person of either sex was unique.[2]

The reason that gold seekers were young men is not difficult to understand. Many chroniclers and journalists, describing events of the earliest days and advising potential immigrants, were careful to point out the hazards of the journey, the dangers involved in the search for gold, and the need for youth, health, and adaptability in seeking the new El Dorado. The great bulk of gold seekers, moreover, came out with the same purposes in mind: to brave the hazards of the journey by land or sea; to spend as short a time as possible scooping up the golden nuggets; and to return home to live on the wealth they had acquired. Very few immigrants intended to make California their home.

The migratory and temporary nature of the population, plus the critical shortage of women in California, contributed to the economic opportunities for prostitutes. Men were arriving in large numbers. Expecting hardships, most left their families at home. The businesswomen—prostitutes—came not to dig for gold in the Sierra but to practice their profession in the city where that gold was spent. They took advantage of the loneliness of the men, the financial rewards, and above all, of the suspension of social and moral restraints.

Of course, prostitutes were not the only ones to recognize the potential for wealth in San Francisco. Those who had rushed to the gold fields in the spring of 1848 (and returned home when the rains started in the fall) discovered that the merchants who had stayed behind were making enormous profits on the first wave of immigrants. Demand had so outdistanced supply that prices were high and going higher every day. Laborers, willing to take any employment six months earlier, suddenly found themselves as valuable a commodity as the precious ore everyone coveted.

During the fall of 1848, a public meeting was called in San Francisco to fix the price of gold at sixteen dollars an ounce.[3] By 1849, the minimum a laborer received for carrying a trunk from the dock to a hotel or a crate to a merchant was one ounce of gold. Arriving in San Francisco in October of 1849 with ten dollars in his pocket (which he promptly lost gambling) Charles Howe tried to get a fifty-cent credit for a meal at a restaurant, and was refused. An hour later, he carried a pork barrel to that same restaurant, demanded twenty dollars for his labor, and was paid without protest.[4] Nor was this an isolated incident. Throughout 1849 and 1850, wages, prices, and profits skyrocketed.

What had not kept pace with the growth of the population was municipal service. Housing and food were grossly inadequate. City services, including police and fire protection—San Francisco was leveled by fire five times between 1849 and 1851—simply did not exist. "Society . . . was in a state of utter disorganization, which became worse and more terrible as the autumn and winter months brought new thousands of immigrants upon the place."[5]

Hotels and restaurants housed in canvas tents charged premium rates. The cost of an ordinary meal fluctuated between $3.50 and $5, with delicacies such as one egg, one potato, or one serving of cabbage selling for one dollar apiece. A blanket and a corner of a hotel bedroom floor, shared with as many as ten other occupants, went for $1.50 a night. For two weeks during the summer a forty-niner could rent a small individual tent for $150—if he was lucky enough to find one. As the season progressed, men would pay even more outrageous prices for any kind of shelter, one going so far as to pay "an ounce [of gold] a week for the privilege of sleeping on a gambling house floor, to be out of the rain and mud." Of the few private rooms available, the cheapest was $200 to $300 a month, and the best brought in $500 to $1,000, "payable in advance."[6]

Workers were not only in great demand and able to command inflated salaries (to meet inflationary expenses), they also improved their image with prestigious titles. Washerwomen were "clothing refreshers" and charged twenty dollars for a dozen pieces; "baggage conveyors and transporters" received two dollars a bag; waiters, addressed as "mister steward," were paid thirty dollars a day; and the formerly common prostitutes of New York or New Orleans became $200- to $500-a-night *"filles de joie."* The average miner, however, was making only $10 to $15 a day, leading many immigrants to conclude that they could get a greater share of the profits without leaving the city. "It was certainly great country, this," the *Annals of San Francisco* recorded. "Every subject was as lofty, independent, and seemingly as rich as a king."[7]

Obviously, everyone was not growing rich, nor was everyone lofty and independent, but to the new arrivals, potential and real success seemed to be in the atmosphere of San Francisco. Their first days in the city may have been made horrendous by rain, fog, mud, and even the cholera that spread briefly in 1849 and 1850, but in their memoirs and recollections of those early days, the image that was remembered was of frantic and profitable activity. Streets were being surveyed and laid out; shops, hotels, storehouses, and saloons were being built—albeit half wood, half canvas—in a matter of days, not weeks. Whole sand hills were moved to fill in the miry places and make room for new buildings and "every body made money, and was suddenly growing rich."[8] An often-repeated account tells of a merchant who, unable to find storage space for his goods, threw them in the mud to use as a foundation for his new building and bewailed the loss a few months later, when the merchandise in the crates holding up his building was worth more on the open market than the entire structure.[9] "No land ever lay beneath the sun which so favored the natural speculator," one observer remarked. And it might be added, without exaggeration, that some form of speculation became the common practice of every resident of San Francisco.[10]

Every bit a part of this world were the prostitutes, who according to the *Annals* brought about a definite improvement. Excitement had been generated by gambling, drinking, and speculation, but when women began to join the crowd,

> *Then a new phase of society appeared. Then reason tottered, and passion ran riot. The allurement of the Cyprian contested the sceptre with the faro bank; champagne at ten dollars a bottle sold as readily in certain localities [parlor houses], as did brandy at fifty cents a glass in the saloon. . . . Dust was plentier than pleasure, pleasure more enticing than virtue. . . . Let none wonder that the time was the best ever made.*[11]

Hubert Bancroft, the nineteenth-century California historian, thought that in no other place had women been so idolized; "it mattered not so much to [the forty-niners] who or what she was; she might be chaste and fair or as wicked as Jezebel."[12] It can hardly be wondered that this was a heady time for women. Yet, no matter how women might view themselves, they had to contend, always, with the opinions of the community where they worked. Ladies were the custodians of society's morals; they were the representatives of everything pure and high-minded and "good." Ladies were the civilizing influence on men. In contrast to them were the other women—the prostitutes.[13]

Despite their unacknowledged position in society, prostitutes have always performed a necessary role, but it was never to be confused with the duties of respectable women. Justifiably or not, prostitution was usually linked with crime. When reformers demanded that municipal authorities reform conditions in the city, the cry was to clean up crime and vice. When a police chief or district attorney was campaigning for reelection, he acquired public support by raiding "houses of ill-fame." And society's impressive social functions were barred to prostitutes, though their customers were always welcome. But such was not the case in those first golden years (1849-1852) in San Francisco. Prostitutes found themselves not only admired as women but respected and uniquely respectable. Hats were removed and bows executed as they passed on the street, they were mentioned politely in the press, and at the first piano concert in June of 1849, they were welcomed to the front seats in the schoolhouse to hear "Jeems Pipes of Pipesville."[14]

In the early period, the prostitutes were businesslike as well as respectable; they made the most of their financial possibilities, and they undoubtedly also enjoyed their social status. The arrival of wives and families in San Francisco would eventually bring a modified version of eastern ways to the West, but until that time, many prostitutes were able in large measure to control their life-style, the cost of their services, and the conditions of their employment.

However, since high profits could also be made in gambling houses, some prostitutes worked in them, reinforcing society's conviction that prostitution belonged to the criminal element. Ignored was the fact that most residents of the city could also be found at the gaming tables. Speculation was a way of life in San Francisco, and its most visible form—gambling—became the city's trademark, as countless games went on twenty-four hours a day.

Gamblers, often accompanied by prostitutes, were among the first of the professional speculators to arrive in California. Like everyone else who managed to reach the state early in 1849, the gambler opened his first establishment in a canvas tent, its front flap wide open, lights blazing, music playing—if musicians could be hired—luring the miner or laborer or businessman inside to try his luck at the tables. By the fall of 1849, "Gambling was a peculiar feature of San Francisco. . . . It was the amusement—the grand occupation of many classes—apparently the life and soul of the place. There were hundreds of gambling saloons in the town."[15]

If a gambler did not have the means to buy land and build

a structure of his own, he often rented space for a table in someone else's establishment. But as "men had come to California for gold; and, by hook or by crook" intended to get it, any reasonably talented professional was quickly able to afford his own saloon.[16] The first permanent structures in the town, and by far the most elegant, were the gambling halls. The most successful were those with women, "beautiful and well-dressed," to deal the cards or turn the roulette wheel, "while lascivious pictures hung on the walls." The miners' lives were harsh and rugged; when they made a strike and came to town they wanted to "celebrate" at the gaming tables with women and drink.[17]

Every observer at the time, no matter how disapproving of gambling, took care to describe the saloons. Three characteristics impressed nearly all: the elegance of the rooms; the complacency of the clientele about any change of fortune; and the presence of women either employed at the gambling tables or merely attending the gamblers.[18] As the city grew and the population increased, the "aristocratic saloons" begun in 1849 and 1850 became more lavish and palatial, with gas lighting, plate glass, and elaborate and expensive ornamentation:

> *In the bar-rooms, there are large plate glass mirrors, alternating with fine paintings in the panels of the walls. There are exquisitely chiseled vases, always containing brilliant and fragrant bouquets of flowers. There are statuettes, and ornamental carving; there are silver and cut glass goblets; there are counters and tables of the finest marble, carved in artistic designs and smoothly polished; the floors are formed of marble tiles, the ceilings finely frescoed, and the windows are of heavy plate glass, ornamented with graceful designs, and the light swinging doors are covered in elegant style and upon the outer door side is a silver door-plate with the name of the proprietor or saloon engraved there on.*[19]

The El Dorado on the Plaza (Portsmouth Square) was the first and longest lived of the glittering establishments, and it had many imitators until public gambling began to diminish after the state legislature passed the Act to Prohibit Gaming

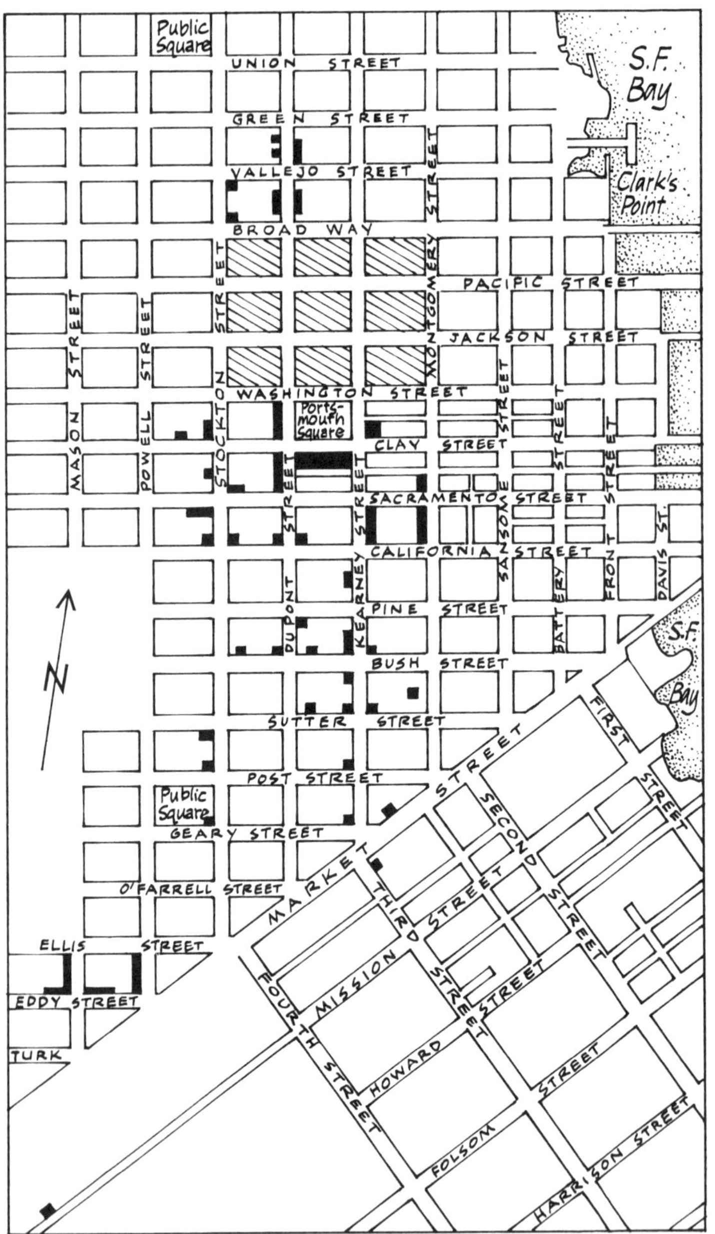

San Francisco in 1853. Diagonal lines indicate the Barbary Coast, and black rectangles locate houses of prostitution in other areas.

in 1855. Neither this Act nor those that followed put an end to gambling itself; the practice merely took on a semiprivate nature, generating a wider gap between elegant saloons and "sordid dens."[20]

While gaming was still public, however, saloons all vied for the same customers, making no attempt to appeal to any specific class of customer, as they did in later years. There was no visible way to differentiate between the rich and the poor, and the saloons were not going to take the chance of missing out on anyone's gold. Most men wore wool shirts and work boots; the unshaven, unwashed miner "who had just come down from the mines" might well be the one who "would put onto a card a great big bag of gold dust, the earnings of months, perhaps, and would lose it all, and walk off complacently."[21] And the well-dressed man complete with boiled white shirt and polished shoes might well be a professional gambler passing time in the saloon while he waited for the opportunity to make his own fortune. Not many years later, a man's dress was a mark of his economic or social standing, but in the early days it was almost a badge of dignity to dress in the practical work clothes of a miner.

The opposite was true of the prostitutes, who were the most elegantly dressed women in San Francisco. Both on the street and in the gambling saloons where they worked, they took great care to be as fashionable as possible. They were the ones, in fact, who set the style for the "ladies" in the city. The largest business expense for the prostitute was her wardrobe, but, as her appearance generally determined much of her earning capacity, it was a necessary expense. Most prostitutes made their contacts in the gambling halls. There was competition among them, however, for employment in the more popular and lavish saloons, which demanded an attractive appearance.[22]

Proprietors of all the lesser-known houses understood that to compete with establishments like the El Dorado on the Plaza, or the Arcade on Commercial Street, they would have to attract women. As one journalist observed in 1850:

> *Women, who are chosen from among the most attractive, are employed to take care of the gambling tables, and naturally [the] men gather in a circle around them.*

> *How can you resist the smile of a lovely lady who invited you? There was a house which they [the gamblers] used not to frequent, and which is doing a* brilliant business *since white hands are rolling the dice, dealing with cards, or turning the wheel of fortune.*[23]

The "lovely ladies" who turned the cards had good reason to smile, since they had the possibility of two incomes. They were paid "high wages to decoy and entertain customers" at the gambling tables; as "waiter-girls" they served food and drink or merely stood beside the men as they gambled. In addition, they were free to make whatever arrangements they chose with individual customers once their shifts were over. Very often, as an added inducement to attract the women, the proprietors would give them the use of private rooms in the same building or rent them to the customers for short periods. This competition among women for positions in the most elegant saloons and among proprietors for women in the cheaper establishments was the initial step in the development of a hierarchy among San Francisco prostitutes; but it was not until 1852 or after that it was possible to differentiate the various classes within the profession. Until that time, the women for the most part worked for themselves on a more or less equal basis—a few even running their own barrooms or gambling saloons.[24]

With the arrival of an additional two thousand females in San Francisco in 1850, many of whom would enlarge the numbers of professionals, it was obvious that competition would soon increase among women rather than for them. As the city began to stabilize both physically and socially after 1851, with more permanent structures and a less-transient population, the more practical and farsighted prostitutes secured what permanency was available to them while conditions were favorable. Some married. Others exchanged the position of a common prostitute for that of a mistress (the more enterprising managed to become the "exclusive" mistress of two or three men), and in this role many former saloon girls amassed fortunes from their "admiring dupes." But most of the true professionals sought to reach the top of the institution's hierarchy by opening their own parlor house or at least becoming a resident in one of the better houses.

III. "THE FAIRER SEX": AMERICAN STYLE

Prostitutes coming to San Francisco in the first decade following the gold rush were professionals. Since the definition of a professional is one who follows an occupation as a profession and raises one's trade to the dignity of a profession, the requirements for a professional prostitute include full-time commitment to her occupation and a conscious effort to maintain or improve her place in the institution. In 1849 and 1850 the city's lack of standard social mores gave each the opportunity to be as entrepreneurial as she chose.

Between 1851 and 1856, however, prostitution in San Francisco was divided into the four categories found in most major cities in the nineteenth century: parlor-house residents, brothel prostitutes, dance-hall harlots, and streetwalkers. Before that, only parlor-house prostitution could be clearly observed. Given the opportunities of the frontier, the fact that the elite segment of the profession was the first to secure its position was not surprising.

Professional prostitutes who traveled on their own to California were coming to improve their position. The primary goal was to acquire a fortune, but the opportunity to upgrade their social or business standing was also available. In more established cities, the parlor house offered greater earnings from higher fees as well as an atmosphere of comfort and elegance. Those who recognized that the unique position they held at the moment was due to the less-restrictive lifestyle of the western frontier sought to secure a place in the elite sector of the profession. Common business sense dictated this ambition, for from London to New Orleans the parlor house was traditionally the most desirable place to work, requiring, as it did, the highest standards of professionalism.

In San Francisco, as elsewhere, the parlor-house resident had to be not only beautiful but accomplished. A visit to a perfectly managed parlor house was much like a visit to a private home, and the prostitutes in residence resembled, in decorum and dress, the daughters of the house. Some writers wittily argued that the only difference, in fact, was that the prostitute was more attractive, more intelligent, and more accomplished than the young society lady.[1]

Visitors, usually "influential gentlemen of the city," would be conducted to a parlor by the madam or a maid. If the customer was not calling on a specific woman, one was chosen by the madam and sent to join him. In the reception room, he would generally find other businessmen and acquaintances being entertained by equally lovely and decorous young women. Witty and intelligent conversation was required of the prostitute, and when necessary the madam would school her in behavior and repartee. Occasionally one of the residents would play the piano, or there might be games of chance for the amusement of the visitor. A supper with all the delicacies San Francisco could offer was served to the guest free, but a charge of ten dollars was added to the customer's bill for every bottle of wine or champagne that he could be induced to purchase. In the very best houses everything was "conducted with the utmost propriety," and any hint of commercialism was kept to a minimum. When the customer was eventually conducted to an elegantly furnished bedroom by the prostitute of his choice, it was usually the madam or a maid who collected the fees, in order to maintain the social distinction between parlor house and commercial brothel, where the prostitute had to collect her own fee.[2]

The very term *parlor house* was to remain an apt description until the Red-light Abatement Act was put into effect in 1914, and houses of prostitution of all descriptions were systematically closed down throughout the city. Until then, the inhabitants of the parlor house appeared to be "ladies," and their place of business appeared to be the same as the other homes in the residential areas where they were found. During the first ten years or so, these other residences were usually boarding houses, which tended to make the parlor houses even less visible than they would be toward the end of the century. The true parlor house was never found in a well-known red-light district, such as the notorious Barbary Coast, because to locate there would have been a contradiction of the image of elegant and refined "respectability."[3]

The interior decor of a typical parlor house usually surpassed the other homes in the neighborhood for luxury. White lace curtains and damask drapes covered the windows. The fixtures and furniture were plush and opulent, and in the early 1850s few people other than the parlor-house madam had the inclination or the incentive to spend time and money on a residential dwelling. But in order to attract a wealthy and influential clientele, it was as necessary for the madam to supply refined elegance in the surroundings as in the women she hired.[4]

To maintain the necessary image, run a house inhabited by ten to twenty young women, and attract sufficient customers to assure profits for both the house and the prostitutes took considerable skill and executive ability. Not all madams were successful. The successful madam seldom worked as a prostitute herself, because to do so would have placed her in competition with her employees, possibly causing dissent among them.

In some houses, the residents paid the madam a flat fee for rooms and additional charges for maid and laundry services, medical treatment, and bribes to the police to assure protection from arrest during periods when vice was the target of municipal reform. In other houses, the madam took care of all financial transactions and kept a percentage of the prostitutes' income. In both cases, considerable bookkeeping skill was required to keep the accounts balanced and avoid conflicts. In some instances, madams might own or run more than one house, which demanded even more managerial ability. They also had to deal with dressmakers to make sure their employees were stylish and well dressed, to bargain with food and wine merchants to guarantee their standards of excellence were met, and to bring in new faces regularly to replace those whose popularity had declined.[5]

In addition to all of these necessary functions, it was the madam's responsibility to attract customers within the bounds of decorum and good taste required of the parlor-house image. One acceptable method of advertising, which became a successful parlor-house custom throughout the century, was the soiree. The first of these functions on record in San Francisco took place in 1849. Elisha Crosby (assigned to set up the judicial branch of government in the new state) recorded in his memoirs that a noted courtesan of the city, called the Countess, maintained a two-story frame house on Washington Street across from the Plaza. Her method of advertising was to send out engraved invitations to the "most prominent men in San Francisco." According to Crosby, when the men arrived they somehow understood that "a gratuity was to be left with the bookkeeper—not less than an ounce ($16) and as much as the liberality of the guest might suggest." Because the Countess had only six or eight young ladies in her employ, she invited others "from the few demimonde houses then in operation." The reception was "very correct, nothing rude, everything refined and elegant, and it was astonishing to see the class of men who gathered there—executive, legislative, judicial, commercial, ministerial, all of what are commonly considered the upper class of society."[6]

At a soiree the best suppers were served and the best wines sold at 500 percent profit. The entire evening often cost the madam a thousand dollars (she was usually able to recoup this expense by the sale of wine or from the customers who chose to spend the night), but it was a necessary expense to advertise her house and a convenient method of introducing a newly hired prostitute to regular customers who might otherwise switch their patronage to another house for variety's sake.[7]

Another successful means of advertising was the daily promenade. As San Francisco became an established city with wooden or brick sidewalks and streets, there were fashionable promenades where ladies could be seen strolling or driving past in carriages. In San Francisco, many of the ladies were part of the demimonde, using the fashionable hour of the promenade to advertise their presence.[8]

Visibility was a necessary aspect in all segments of the trade, and since they had entree to public entertainments, the prostitutes attended the few social events available outside the gambling halls. Since there were very few families in San Francisco and even fewer homes, private parties were rare (even in the late 1850s gatherings in private homes or apartments where a hostess was present were so scarce that they called for special mention in letters and journals); but public lectures, plays, concerts, and balls were favorite San Francisco pastimes. Virtually the only "society" articles in the newspapers before 1852 were reports of attendance at these public affairs, especially dances and balls at new hotels such as the Parker House, or social events sponsored by groups like the Monumental Fire Company. According to the *Alta California,* May 24, 1849, such affairs were attended by "the staid matron and quiet maid" as well as "the beauteous gazelle-eyed maidens of Alta California." The public balls attracted both the fair and the frail of the female population, and there was very little condemnation of manners and decorum. The masked balls, on the other hand, led many writers to warn against the dangers that anonymity might lead to. It was feared masks might make some women feel liberated from moral restraints.[9]

As the numbers of women in San Francisco increased, the grand ball gradually became restricted until ladies were admitted only by an invitation card.[10] But the masked or masquerade balls remained open to all, and the *Alta California* reported that they were "recherché affairs."

> *By the private entrance come the maskers, male and female. The Spanish bandit, with his high tapering hat, ornamented with ribbons; the gipsy, with her basket and cards; the Bloomer, bountiful in short skirts and satin-covered extremities; the ardent young militaire . . . the flaunting Cyprian, not veiled by domino or mask; and the curious, but* respectable *lady, hidden by cloak and false visage. There is the Frenchman in a fantastical dress; and Gallic count imitating the Yankee; the Yankee affecting "Aunty Vermont"; and men*

> *already feeling the force of their libations affecting sobriety. . . .*
>
> *Away they whirl through the waltz, or dash along the mazourka, or crash away promiscuously in the gallapade. Where there are no masks exercise brings no new rose tint or crimson to the soft cheek—the rouge or carmine is too thick for that. The music draws to a close and ends with a grand flourish. Off to the bar and coffee stand go the maskers, the gentlemen to treat, the others to be treated.*[11]

With drink came violent encounters among men and women. "Jealousy's eyes take a greener tinge from the bottle imp, and woman, forgetting her last prerogative—gentleness—joins the ring and gives point and effect to feminine oaths by the use of feminine nails."[12]

Recherché or not, such functions remained a popular pastime in San Francisco, and the high attendance by "flaunting Cyprians" was probably surpassed only by their numbers at the Prostitutes Ball sponsored by the proprietor of the Music Hall.[13]

The very fact that the event was advertised as a prostitutes ball is an indication of the change taking place in the demimonde of San Francisco by 1856. In the first year or two of the decade, euphemisms for prostitutes were the *fair but frail* or *ladies in full bloom.* By 1853, however, more derogatory terms like *prostitute, cyprian, harlot,* and even *whore* were used more frequently. There are two obvious explanations for the change in status. First, wives and families were arriving in San Francisco in sufficient numbers to insist on exclusive rights to respectability. Second, the number of prostitutes in San Francisco had grown sufficiently (some estimate there were two thousand by 1853) to make it impossible for all to be able to maintain the more admired status of courtesan. There were, in fact, cyprians, bawds, and even whores among the professional prostitutes.[14]

As members of the profession began to separate into more traditional categories within the institution, so did their places of employment and the range of their economic opportunities.[15] The parlor-house resident offered illusion along with sex in order to attract her wealthy clientele; her income, accordingly, was at the top of the scale. The brothel prostitutes, for the most part, dispensed with lavish elegance, and although they could not command the same fees as the parlor-house resident, their expenses for accommodations and wardrobe were less. A few brothels were nearly as elegant as a parlor house, the only difference being lower fees, a poorer quality of wine, and a madam whose requirements for decorum and appearance were less stringent. Most were cheap boarding houses, rented exclusively to prostitutes and run by a landlord or landlady.

The dance-hall harlot, on the other hand, had to rely on quantity rather than quality to assure her income. She met her customers in dance halls (sometimes a synonym for cheap gambling saloons or barrooms), and if the hall did not provide cubicles or back rooms for her use, she often used her own room in a hotel or boarding house or rented a room in one of the "large and flimsily built houses called 'cribs'," built exclusively for prostitution, "consisting of many small rooms" opening onto a street or alley, where the prostitute could solicit customers as they passed.[16] The *WASP*, a San Francisco weekly newspaper, described the scene on September 20, 1876: "God-forsaken women are permitted to stand in their doors and windows dressed, or rather 'undressed,' in the most shameful manner, inviting men and boys to enter their vile dens." Cribs contained anywhere from 15 to 160 rooms; some were run like hotels, where the women simply rented the rooms by the night to conduct their business; others had managers who recruited prostitutes.

Brothels between these two extremes appeared to be simple boarding houses. The structures were not distinctive and were often found next door to a private residence. In a two-block area of the sixth ward, for example, there were ten brothels housing thirty-four prostitutes. In the midst of this bevy of sexual industry lived a steel contractor and his family and a minister of the Reformed Church and his wife. The landlady or landlord of these brothels was a cross between a madam and a crib manager and was usually an employee (as was the crib manager) rather than the owner. The owners were often small groups of businessmen or municipal officials who could afford to buy city property at the inflated prices of the 1850s and 1860s. One brothel on Jackson Street was actually called the Municipal Crib, because both patrons and owners were the politicians and officials of the city. As competition increased, brothel prostitutes had less choice in their place of employment and therefore less opportunity to improve their position in the hierarchy.[17]

Cheap brothels and cribs were usually found in the Barbary Coast, a nine-block area bounded by Montgomery Street on the east, Stockton Street on the west, Broad Way on the north, and Washington Street on the south. It grew up around the nucleus of Sydney Town and Little Chile at the foot of Telegraph Hill but did not become a notorious red-light district until after 1865. The heart of the Barbary Coast was Pacific Street, the most notorious street was Kearney, and the Chinese district was on Dupont (Grant Street). Bars, dance halls, cribs, and dives crowded the area, and every conceivable source of crime, vice, and entertainment was to be found.

Because private accommodations in San Francisco remained scarce in and out of the Barbary Coast through the 1870s, many boarding houses and hotels rented to both prostitutes and nonprostitutes. The St. Francis Hotel, for example, listed a number of prostitutes as residents, along with the typical transient clientele. Boarding houses throughout the fourth, sixth, and eighth wards (roughly the central area of the city) housed anywhere from two to ten prostitutes as well as laborers, bartenders, gamblers, and the like. The brothel run by Eli and Kate Calli in the fourth ward also rented rooms to three machinists. Women unable to find a place in a brothel or crib worked out of their own rooms, which they might share with their children, husband, or mother. Brothel keepers, as opposed to parlor-house madams, usually lived with their families in the brothel. The problem of finding a permanent place in a brothel or desirable accommodation of any kind increased with each decade, particularly for the dance-hall harlot.[18]

Dance-hall work after 1856 was actually an extension of gambling-saloon work and barroom work, which was what most prostitutes did in 1849–1850. Gambling itself was becoming less visible, although in the clubs that continued to flourish women were still hired as waiter girls to serve drinks and food, some to dance or sing on stage, and, in the dives or beer joints, to dance with customers for twenty-five cents a dance. In clubs like the Bella Union, the Olympic, and Gilbert's Melodeon, all in the heart of the Barbary Coast, gambling was available, stage shows added to the festivities, and on a mezzanine, in private boxes that could be curtained off, waiter girls would provide sex as well as food and drink. At Hell's Kitchen and the Opera Comique there was less luxury in the surroundings, but the second floor was divided into cubicles for the convenience of customers and the forty "pretty waiter-girls" hired to serve them.[19]

The dance-hall harlot who had to provide her own room very often did not receive a salary for her presence in the dive where she found customers. She was, in fact, San Francisco's version of a streetwalker or whore. Until the Red-light Abatement Act closed houses of prostitution in every category, streetwalkers were few in number and were clearly the worst paid and least professional members of the institution. During the Barbary Coast era (1865–1914) the streetwalkers did most of their soliciting in the dives and cheap barrooms that did not hire their own harlots. It was women in this category who occasionally showed up on police arrest records as common prostitutes, while brothel and crib prostitutes, when arrested, were charged with the misdemeanor of "soliciting for a house of ill-fame." There were also occasional arrests for keeping a house of ill fame and for being an inmate of a house of ill fame, but these were associated with the lower-class brothels and cribs. Although the parlor-house residents and their madams were among the best-known women in the city, they were almost never arrested.[20]

Well-known madams of San Francisco appear in memoirs and records throughout the nineteenth century. One apparent favorite of the 1890s was Tessie Wall. Many anecdotes have been told about Tessie, but the one which best reflects a madam's business abilities and class consciousness is the one about Gump's Jade and Oriental Art Emporium. Tessie's parlor house on O'Farrell Street was furnished with the traditional elegance of such establishments, so it was not unusual for her to order a thousand-dollar painting from this exclusive store. When one of the younger Gump sons delivered the painting, he and Tessie celebrated with a bottle of champagne. When he returned to the store, however, he carried only $990. Tessie had deducted $10 for the wine from the sale price of the painting![21]

Another regular customer of Gump's was May Stuart, also a well-known madam. When her bill at the store reached $500, one of the Gump sons visited her and politely requested payment. May readily acknowledged her debt, promised to pay as quickly as possible, and as collateral showed him the sleeping form of the "scion of one of the old families." She paid her bill in full the following day.[22]

Tessie and May's place in San Francisco society seemed reasonably safe and accepted, because they did not flaunt their occupation. Generally, only the open vice of the Barbary Coast aroused outcries from religious and reform groups. At the beginning of the period—the early 1850s—two other famous madams did flaunt their lifestyle, and the usually tolerant frontier society rose up against them. No women so clearly depict the changing status of the prostitute in the first decade after the gold rush as do Irene McCready and Belle Cora.

Irene arrived in San Francisco in April 1849 with her lover and business partner, James McCabe. McCabe had been a successful businessman in the East, and he was able to increase his wealth in San Francisco. He was co-owner of the El Dorado and apparently helped his mistress set up one of the earliest bagnios in the city. He also helped her to rebuild it in keeping with the ideal of the parlor house after the fire of December 1849 destroyed both the house and the El Dorado.[23]

During her first year in San Francisco, Irene and the other women in her occupation were in effect the *haut ton* of female society. As one forty-niner later claimed, "the commonest proverb in the street was that the only aristocracy we had here at the time were the gamblers and prostitutes; and it was true too."[24] But Irene was, perhaps, not astute enough to realize that her position was the result of unique circumstances. Consequently, it must have come as a distinct and unwelcome surprise to learn that the men who bowed to her in the street or paid her elaborate compliments when they visited her house would ask her to leave a gathering that included their wives.

The incident involving Irene and the few "respectable" ladies of the town occurred sometime in 1850 and was perhaps the first time the security of the prostitute's status was tested. A dozen or so ladies from four churches in the city, including Sara Royce (who left us an account of the incident), had organized a benevolent society and held an "entertainment" to raise funds for their charitable work. In the midst of the tea-party-like atmosphere "a man [McCabe], prominent for wealth and business-power," entered with his mistress, Irene. She was, Royce explained, "a splendidly dressed woman, well known in the city as the disreputable companion of her wealthy escort." At their wives' insistence, a delegation of men asked McCabe to leave with the famous madam, because the ladies refused to associate with her or have her introduced to their daughters.[25] The confrontation was undoubtedly a result of Irene's inflated self-confidence. Nevertheless, the incident does reflect the view some prostitutes had developed of their position in San Francisco society.

It was another five years before the presence of the demimonde society was challenged at a public function. If Irene displayed her presence because of unrealistic self-confidence in her acceptability, Belle Cora flaunted her position fully conscious of the reaction she would create. She made the challenge and expected to win. Bancroft, who treated prostitutes sympathetically in his writings though he deplored the institution, described her thus:

> *Like Cleopatra, she was very beautiful, and, beside the power that comes of beauty, rich; but oh, so foul. Flaunting her beauty and wealth on the gayest thoroughfares, and on every gay occasion, with senator, judge, and citizen at her beck and call, and being a woman as proud as she was beautiful and rich, she not infrequently flung back upon her stainless sisters the looks of loathed contempt with which they so often favored her.*[26]

Like Irene and many of the other early prostitutes and madams, Belle was the mistress of a gambler. She had accompanied Charles Cora to San Francisco in 1849, and during 1850 and probably 1851, they spent most of their time in the mining towns of Sacramento, Sonora, and Marysville.

Charles gambled, with apparently mixed success; Belle opened at least one bagnio in Sonora and was as successful as she was to be with all the houses she owned. In 1852 they were back in San Francisco, and Belle started her career as the city's most successful madam by opening a parlor house on Dupont Street. By 1855 she had at least two houses, the second being a two-story brick structure on Waverly Place. It was in November of 1855, while she and Charles were enjoying the economic rewards of their respective professions, that Belle confronted "respectable" society. Unlike Irene, Belle won her battle, but Charles paid the price at the end of a vigilante rope.[27]

As they had done many times before, Belle and Charles attended a play at the American Theater. Seated directly in front of them were United States Marshal W. H. Richardson and his wife. When Mrs. Richardson realized who was behind her, she insisted her husband tell them to leave. The Coras refused. Richardson called the manager of the theater, demanding the Coras be evicted. The manager also refused to comply. In the end it was the Richardsons who left the theater, while Belle kept her seat in triumph. But two days later, Cora and Richardson confronted each other in a saloon, quarrelled (presumably over the theater incident), and before witnesses could be sure of the actual course of events, Cora had shot the marshal. He was very quickly arrested for murder.[28]

Belle might conceivably have regretted her victory over the virtuously outraged Mrs. Richardson but, unlike that lady, she did not succumb to vapors and tears. Her first action was to use a substantial portion of her wealth to hire the best criminal defense lawyers in San Francisco. There was sufficient evidence to suggest that Cora had shot Richardson in self-defense. But Belle was a realist: Charles might be convicted because he was a gambler with a notorious madam as his mistress and because Richardson was a United States marshal. Unwilling to take chances, Belle used additional funds to bribe various witnesses and some members of the jury. Such practices were not unusual in San Francisco, but unfortunately for Cora the bribes were discovered. The prosecution and the press had a field day with this "proof of guilt." Nevertheless, Colonel Edward Baker, Cora's lawyer, managed to convince at least some of the jury that self-defense was a possibility, and when they were unable to reach a unanimous verdict, Cora was held over for a second trial.

Because of Belle's attempted bribes, Baker was forced to defend her actions, and his remarks to the jury might be read as the first legal testimony to the existence of the prostitute with a heart of gold. Belle Cora, Baker told the jury, might have been misguided in her bribery attempts but she was only trying to help her friend. "It is a woman of base profession, of more than easy virtue, of malign fame, of a degraded caste—it is one poor, weak, feeble, and, if you like it, wicked woman—to her alone he owes his ability to employ counsel to present his defense." Charles and Belle might not have conformed to the standards of society or been sanctioned by the church, but "they were bound together by a tie which angels might not blush to approve. A bad woman may lose her virtue; it would be infinitely worse to lose her faith according to her own standards. . . . If any of you have it in your heart to condemn, and say 'Stand back! I am holier than thou,' remember Magdalene."[29]

Baker's eloquence was sufficient to save Cora from a legal hanging, but on May 23, 1856, the second vigilance committee took him from the jail, gave him a second "trial," and hanged him. Always punctilious on the etiquette governing a prisoner's last request, the committee allowed Cora, a Catholic, the services of a priest. And when Archbishop Allemany "refused to grant him absolution, unless he first married the woman he had been living with so long as his wife," the committee brought Belle from Waverly Place, and she was legally united with the man whose name she had used for so long.[30]

Belle had not bowed to defeat when Charles was arrested, nor did she do so when she became his widow. On the contrary, true to the description Bancroft wrote of her later, she continued to flaunt herself before her "stainless sisters," promenading on the city's thoroughfares and maintaining her luxurious parlor house on Waverly Place until her death in 1862. Even Irene, though she had to retire from the presence of "respectability," continued her successful career for many years. But the life of a madam, though requiring a keen business sense, was physically less taxing than that of the majority of women in the profession.

Very simply, for women in any category of prostitution to move upward in the profession required beauty, financing, the desire and ability to maintain professional standards, and self-discipline. Downward mobility resulted from the failure to maintain any one of these requirements. Beauty is, of course, not something that can be controlled, especially in a profession that requires late hours that are physically taxing. Also, if a woman was not sufficiently professional to maintain self-discipline, she very often used alcohol or drugs to sustain herself. The result was usually the decline of her status in the hierarchy.[31]

There were other causes for downward mobility, not the least of which was venereal disease and unwanted pregnancies, constant dangers in the profession. There are no statistics on pregnancy among prostitutes, but in reform literature and benevolent society tracts the problem of abandoned and unwanted children was a continuing subject for debate and the object of charitable works. How much birth control was known or practiced among prostitutes is also unknown, but police and court reports show occasional arrests of abortionists throughout the nineteenth century.[32]

Losing one's place in a brothel because of pregnancy, however, did not mean retiring from the profession. In the 1870 census, which lists prostitution as an occupation, many women on the rolls had their child or children living with them. In some cases they worked as entrepreneurial prostitutes in their own home; in other cases, they rented rooms in a brothel and left the child with a sitter or relative. Pregnancy did not automatically mean downward mobility or setting up on one's own, but very few brothels or parlor houses would hold the place of an employee who could not work. Furthermore, in all the kinds of houses, the constant need for new faces made for little job security.

The easiest method to move up in the profession was through a sponsor. If a brothel prostitute or dance-hall harlot could attract the interest of a wealthy or influential man, he could very often use his influence to establish her in his favorite parlor house or in one of the better brothels. Judge McGowan, a notorious character even for San Francisco, not only kept his favorite prostitute in his favorite house but occasionally even lived there with her. Since madams were usually willing to humor their regular customers, the price was probably no more than a new wardrobe for the favorite, one more in keeping with her new surroundings. Whether she kept her new position when her sponsor's interest diminished depended on the vagaries of customer demand, and her age, beauty, and ability to adapt to her new status.[33]

The length of a prostitute's professional life is difficult to estimate. In 1850, one courtesan retired after making $50 thousand in one year. At the other end of the scale is the information in an 1895 almshouse report about a ninety-three-year-old woman who had apparently been a regular inmate of the almshouse, off and on, for a number of years. Her habits were still listed as intemperance and prostitution! Obviously the average prostitute fit neither of these extremes. The census reports list women from their teens to their fifties as working prostitutes. There were mothers and daughters practicing the profession at the same time, but evidence on the length of their career is sketchy and inconclusive. As there was no penicillin to fight syphilis, many died from this occupational disease or from bungled abortions. Some left the profession to take jobs in other occupations open to women in the nineteenth century, such as clerks or domestic workers. The more frugal among them, according to some observers, opened their own dress or hat shops. And still others gave up the profession for marriage.[34] Beyond that point we can only speculate, but it is clear that though the halcyon days for prostitutes in early San Francisco did not continue long, their position in society was never quite as far beyond the pale as it was in the East. Once the day-to-day hardships of building a city were past, the early pioneers romanticized their city, and the demimonde was just as much a part of that romance as the anecdotes of empire building, of overnight millionaires, and of a city that could be raised six times from the ashes like a phoenix.

IV. Filles de Joie: The Cosmopolitan Element

Anglo-American prostitutes were neither the first nor the highest paid in San Francisco. Both of those distinctions belonged to others. Mexican and other Latin American prostitutes were the earliest; they migrated to California with the first wave of gold seekers in 1848. And French prostitutes, who arrived in 1850, commanded the greatest admiration and the highest prices. Australia, China, and Germany also had significant representation among the demimonde. With the notable exception of the French, these foreign women were occasionally the objects of xenophobic attacks from the increasingly nationalistic Americans.

The nationalistic and at times even ethnocentric attitude of the North Americans manifested itself among gold seekers from the eastern states before their first ship reached San Francisco. Among the immigrants in 1849 was a Reverend Samuel Willey, who left New York with a delegation of ministers and missionaries to establish Protestant churches and schools in the newly acquired Mexican territories. The discovery of gold had not been publicized before they sailed in early December. By the time they reached New Orleans, en route to the Isthmus of Panama, the excitement was already widespread. When it left New Orleans, their ship carried an additional two hundred passengers "in a fever to get to the

California mines." Among the new contingent mingling with Willey and the other ministers were some of the gamblers and prostitutes who formed part of the first wave of American gold seekers in early 1849. With some alarm, Willey described them as "the class, most loose of foote who could leave on so short notice." They were not, he worried, people of the sort he was going to California to build schools and churches for but rather "such as frequented the gambling saloons."[1]

When Willey and his fellow passengers had crossed the isthmus and reached the Pacific, the first steamer that arrived in Panama City to take them up the coast to California already carried sixty-nine Peruvian passengers. Because there were more Americans waiting than the ship could carry, the impatient travelers insisted that the Peruvians leave the steamer to make room for them. When this demand was ignored, General Persifor F. Smith, traveling to California to take over the post of military commander, bowed to pressure from the Americans and issued a proclamation that "foreigners would not be allowed to work in the United States gold mines." The proclamation had no legal standing and was clearly unenforceable. The Peruvians still refused to give up their places, but the proclamation somewhat pacified the Americans and forestalled violence. The steamer finally sailed, having taken on twice its capacity of 150 passengers but leaving many behind to await the next ship.[2]

The attitude of Anglo-Americans toward non-Americans in California was generally hostile throughout the remainder of the century. The more violent manifestations of racism were directed against the more visible foreigners, such as Latin Americans and Chinese, but Australians, Irish, and Germans were occasionally the objects of xenophobic prejudice as well. For the most part, violence was directed at the male population, but foreign prostitutes experienced their share of prejudice in the form of contempt or derogatory remarks in the press that American professionals were not subject to until later in the century.[3]

The first to suffer from such public abuse were Mexican and South American women. Most of them took up residence in the town, while the men they traveled with either continued on to the gold fields or stayed with them to set up cheap cantinas and fandango parlors, which provided women, liquor, and gambling to the transient population. The area where they lived and worked, Little Chile, was at the foot of Telegraph Hill.

The gold rush had brought a large criminal element to San Francisco, men and women who "never intended to follow a reputable calling there." The "Hounds" were part of this element, as were the "Sydney Ducks." The Hounds were a group of disbanded veterans from a regiment of New York volunteers who acted for a time as regulators hired by both the government and private parties. Unfortunately—since San Francisco had no regular police force in 1848—they quickly descended to the lawbreaker ranks, taking advantage of their organized position to rob, intimidate, and plunder, primarily in Little Chile. The criminal attacks of the Hounds roused the community to organize a volunteer police force in the summer of 1849 to protect the Chileans, Peruvians, and Mexicans. Nevertheless, the immigrants continued to be vilified by the press and the population at large as the class of foreigners which "was generally of the lowest and most degraded character."[4]

The contemptuous attitude toward Latin Americans was widespread. Other minorities, though held in contempt, were occasionally praised for their politeness, cleanliness, or industry; not so the Latin Americans. Every contemporary account of the inhabitants of Little Chile agreed in substance with the description in the *Annals:*

> *Their habits were unclean and their manners base. The men seemed deceivers by nature, while the women . . . were immodest and impure to a shocking degree. These were washerwomen by day; by night—and, if a dollar could be earned, also by day—they were only prostitutes. Both sexes lived almost promiscuously in large tents. . . . Their dwellings were dens of infamy, where drunkenness and whoredom, gambling, swindling, cursing and brawling, were constantly going on.*[5]

No matter how widely this attitude prevailed, it did not keep customers away from Little Chile. Even the Hounds, who would rob, steal, and assault inhabitants during the day, paid their dollar to the prostitute at night.[6]

But why only a dollar, when any American woman could demand and receive an ounce of gold for an hour of her time? And why were the women of Mexico, Chile, and Peru treated so contemptuously in a town where men would run into the street just to stare at a woman as she passed? Xenophobia, though a factor, is not a sufficient explanation for the position of Latin American women in San Francisco. Neither is intensified race hatred resulting from the War with Mexico a satisfactory answer, though, to be sure, it was a factor, since many forty-niners were veterans of the war. The explanation must rest primarily on an analysis of prostitution itself and on the amount of control the women had over their position.

There were only two non-American groups of professional prostitutes in San Francisco who did not significantly improve their social or economic condition by coming to California: Latin Americans and Chinese. Although individual Chinese or Latin American women might occasionally achieve both financial and social success, most were consistently on the lower steps of the institution's hierarchy. In both cases the cause seems to be that the majority of these women were, in effect, indentured into prostitution.

In the first wave of forty thousand immigrants who came by ship in 1849, seven hundred were women, mostly Latin Americans. In some cases, the women themselves made arrangements with ship captains to carry them to San Francisco, where payment for the trip could be found. More often, however, cantina owners would contract with a captain to recruit women in his ports of call, or possibly send an agent to recruit them, guaranteeing the fare and a commission for the procurer. In the first few years of the gold rush, this was an extensive and lucrative speculative venture. Women, as an importable cargo, offered higher profits and less risk than other commodities. In return for passage, the women usually had to indenture themselves for six months to whoever paid their way.[7] "Hundreds were brought from Mazatlan and San Blas on trust, and transferred to bidders with whom the girls shared their earnings."[8]

The financial improvement in San Francisco must have been sufficient to warrant the move. The fact that they could control neither their place of employment nor their clientele—being forced to spend their first six months in the new frontier working exclusively for someone else—kept them from taking part in the independent and individualistic ways of the new community which led to the economic and social improvements of others. They could not insist on being treated as courtesans when they were hired as whores and harlots and had no other option. Having missed the initial discovery that in San Francisco the opportunity to control the future was there for the taking, the women appeared to be satisfied with a limited improvement in their financial situation, even when the period of indenture was over. The fact that they did not attempt to receive the highest price suggests that they were accustomed to being worth very little where they came from.[9] In the press and in journals they were referred to as "greaseritas", who were abandoned to "disgusting lewd practices, and shameless." And except for those who were able to "pass" as Spanish rather than Mexican, their names were seldom found among the residents of parlor houses or the more expensive brothels.

The status of prostitutes was defined by their clientele and the environment in which they worked and lived. Little Chile was where cantina owners who imported Latin American prostitutes had their establishments. Latin American men also congregated in that area, grouping together because of cultural similarity and because they were subject to racism in other parts of the city. Latin American prostitutes therefore found themselves living in an area cut off from the elegant sections of town. That their surroundings were cheap and tawdry, that they did not speak English, and that they had no opportunity to learn the refinements of parlor-house work also had some influence on their lack of advancement. Most cantina prostitutes shared their profits with owners, and the owners were as interested in the volume of customers at the gaming tables and bar as they were in the prostitutes' customers. How much control the women had over which customers they received is unknown, but it seems likely that they had very little.

Racism also played an important part in the immobility of the Latina prostitute. For the women to have left the cantinas of Pacific Street for the gambling saloons of Portsmouth Square in 1850 and 1851 would have meant attracting a new clientele from among the unpredictable Anglos. The social change must have seemed too risky. There was nothing in the press or the behavior of the populace to suggest to the Latina prostitutes that they would have been accepted.[10]

By the 1870s some Mexican prostitutes did alter their working and living conditions, working throughout the city in apartments and boarding houses as well as in brothels. The 1870 census lists a number of households that arouse speculation on the changing status of Mexican prostitutes. One household included William Wilson, aged forty-nine, born in England, married to Antonia, also forty-nine, born in Mexico, and a daughter Lzetia, aged twenty. Wilson ran a saloon, Antonia kept house, and Lzetia was a prostitute. Pauline Lehana, aged fifty-six, was born in Mexico and kept house for her daughter Elzango, aged thirty-eight, and granddaughter Anita, aged twenty, both prostitutes. Husband-and-wife and mother-and-daughter households were not isolated, nor were they limited to Latina women, but the press used such households as "proof" that Latin American women were "of the vilest character."

The only other group of foreign prostitutes to experience a negative reaction in San Francisco from the earliest days were the Chinese, and they, too, came to San Francisco under an indenture system. Their indenture and the fact that they were racially identifiable by xenophobic white Americans are the only similarities between Latin American and Chinese prostitutes. A few Chinese prostitutes arrived in San Francisco as free agents, and others, like the noted Madam Ah Toy, managed to buy their contracts and set up in business for themselves. But for the most part, young Chinese girls from poor families were sold into prostitution by their fathers or guardians or kidnapped and sold to brothels by professional procurers. In their case, the indenture became the equivalent of enslavement.

The professional procurers for Chinese women were usually members or employees of the Hip Ye Tong, which controlled Chinese prostitution in California. To the Western mind, the Tong's practice was deplorable and the women's condition was excused because it was no fault of their own. The fact that a Chinese woman was "brought from China and farmed out to the highest bidder, who in turn [made] merchandise of her, the woman, having no more control over her moral or even physical condition, often than caged animals" was sufficient cause to give Chinese prostitutes unusual standing within the institution throughout the century.[11]

Before 1851 there were only seven Chinese women known to be in San Francisco (one reportedly a wife). Like other gold seekers, Chinese men had no intention of settling in California and therefore did not bring their families. By 1851, however, the wealthier men contracted with the Tong for "young, beautiful and pure girls" as concubines. Owners or managers of brothels exclusively reserved for Chinese men also contracted for Chinese women. Houses that catered to non-Chinese customers simply requested women. Women were sold on arrival to the highest bidder unless they were brought in for a specific customer. Such sales usually took place on the docks, with the bidding being conducted before spectators, who often included police. Later in the century, when attempts to regulate Chinese immigration included turning away single women who arrived by ship, the procurers hired Chinese residents to meet the newcomers and claim they were sisters, wives, or daughters. Auctions were then conducted in the basements of various Chinatown dives, such as those found in Jones Alley or Sullivan's Alley. Those who had come under contract were turned over to the brothel owner who had ordered them.[12]

It was extremely difficult for Chinese prostitutes to better their situation, and it was an advantage to be purchased to fulfill a specific contract as a concubine or for a Chinese house because it was much easier for members of this elite group to make enough money to buy their freedom than it was for women in the cheaper houses, which catered to non-Chinese customers. Ah Toy, the most famous Chinese prostitute and madam (also believed to be the first Chinese prostitute in San Francisco), however, was one of the few able to move upward in the profession. She bought her first brothel with the help of some of her American clients and contracted with the Tong for her own prostitutes.[13]

Ah Toy (sometimes called Atoy or Achoy), "with her slender body and laughing eyes," was a well-known figure in San Francisco.[14] Unlike most women in her profession and of her race, she did not hesitate to put the American judicial system to work for her. Although prostitutes often lodged complaints against men who abused them physically, once the police arrived and ended the violence, the women were usually satisfied and rarely turned up in court to press charges.[15] "Blooming with youth, beauty and rouge," Ah Toy made one of her frequent appearances in court to prosecute those who "disturbed the order of her disorderly house through attempts to tax the Chinese women." Such attempts were made periodically by other brothel owners offering protection and also by policemen attempting to use city ordinances against prostitution to their own advantage. The *Picayune* publicized this practice, requesting in print that they be informed whether there was a flaw in the ordinance, whether it was only enforced against Chinese women, or whether it was in fact a system for police payoffs.[16]

The championing of Chinese prostitutes by the press in San Francisco was not in fact unique to the *Picayune*. Most newspapers throughout the century, while condemning the "vile dens of Chinese prostitution," excused the women themselves. The *California Police Gazette*, August 20, 1859, reporting the arrest of La You for prostitution, took the opportunity to point out the discrepancies in law enforcement.

> *The usual offense, the usual bail and the usual result: bail forfeited. It is a pity officers could not find some better employment than prosecuting these poor Chinese slaves. Do they not know that these poor serfs are* obliged *to do as they do? The officers do not pitch into WHITE females who pursue the same course. Oh no, they could not do that. Their pleasures and interests would be interfered with.*

When the police announced a "big crackdown" against gambling and prostitution, the *Gazette* again asked why it was only enforced against the Chinese (May 11 and 18, 1867). "The police are certainly deserving of praise," the paper reported sarcastically, after announcing three arrests in an area where fifty gambling and prostitution establishments were known to run openly.

Still later in the century (1880s), at the height of Chinese exclusion activities, even the Workingmen's Party excused the women for "ply[ing] their miserable vocation," because they were "slaves and . . . sold to the proprietors" of dens or to rich merchants for their personal pleasure. The Workingmen's Party, though it "utterly repudiate[d] the idea of being moved by any race prejudice or class hatred" in its activities to exclude the Chinese, declared that the "unscrupulous, lying and treacherous Chinamen" were the cause of most health problems in the city and argued that at least "nine-tenths of the dreadful disease" (syphilis) came from Chinese prostitutes.[17]

The accuracy of the Workingmen's Party statistics may be doubted, but it was a fact that massive overcrowding and poor sanitation made disease in the Chinese section of the city a major problem. It is also a reasonable deduction that syphilis was a major cause of death among Chinese prostitutes.[18] Since their indenture period was usually a matter of years and not months, their chances of contracting venereal disease were great. Also, proprietors of the lower-class dens rarely turned away any customers.

Agitation against the Chinese in California and potential Chinese immigrants was intermittent before 1865, but even then the most frequent argument for exclusion was to stop the spread of disease. In referring specifically to Chinese prostitutes, the motives were often asserted to be humanitarian as well. In 1860, the chief of police reported to the board of supervisors:

> *With regard to Chinese prostitutes, common humanity dictates that a law should be made for the protection of these miserable beings, who, whether sick or well, willing or unwilling, are compelled by their degraded owners, to submit to every pollution dictated by corrupt minds, and sanctioned by the avarice of the keepers of these unfortunates. Words are powerless to point out the condition of loathsome disease in which they exist.*[19]

Despite excuses made for the "miserable beings," it was the Chinese prostitutes, not the importers, owners, or customers, who suffered under police crackdowns against vice. Under the Additional Powers Act given to the city by the state legislature, the board of supervisors in 1865 passed an "Order to remove Chinese women of ill-fame from certain limits in the city."[20] On the advice of the city attorney, the word *Chinese* was removed from the ordinance, but the police were well aware of the fact that Chinese prostitutes were to be the object of the cleanup.

The increased agitation against the Chinese after 1865 was for the most part a reaction against the importation of thousands of Cantonese to build the Central Pacific Railroad across the Sierra. In the work camps there was very little objection to their presence, because they "relieved the white men of pick and shovel work; many whites even advanced to become gang foremen" or more skilled jobs, thus reinforcing, they believed, the dignity and superiority of the Caucasian. In San Francisco, however, labor unions were growing strong, and though their members wanted nothing to do with the hazardous conditions of laying a railroad line across the Sierra, their leaders were influential in molding opinion. The influx of Chinese, willing to work longer hours for lower wages, would, the union leaders predicted, cause economic ruin for California in the future. Periodic acts of indiscriminate violence occurred in the Chinese quarter of town (primarily in the 1870s, but occasionally in the late 1860s as well). Since the agitators were voters and the victims were not, the anti-Chinese reaction of municipal authorities was, perhaps, to be expected.[21]

San Francisco city officials were as subject to xenophobic impulses as anyone else in the city and also felt the need to show their constituents that they were doing something about the "Chinese problem." The railroad workers were out of their province, since they were in another county, but they could endorse stringent enforcement of the vice laws against Chinese gamblers and prostitutes. Consequently, in 1867 fourteen owners of houses of ill fame were arrested—all of them Chinese. In 1869, there were twenty-nine arrests for importing prostitutes—all of them Chinese. In the same fiscal year that the board of supervisors passed their "Order to remove Chinese women of ill-fame . . ." there were 136 women arrested for common prostitution; the previous year there had been one! Their race was not listed, but indications in the police report summaries throughout the century show increased arrests for prostitution in years when anti-Chinese activities were at their peak.[22] The fact that the 136 arrests were politically motivated to get "good press" was ludicrously obvious: the 1870 census listed approximately 1,500 Chinese prostitutes living and working in brothels and cribs in San Francisco's Chinatown.

Despite the violent racism, official harassment of Chinese prostitutes, and the attempts at exclusion, the women continued to receive sympathetic treatment by the press. They also became the favored objects of charitable organizations. The 1880s and 1890s was the era of settlement houses and rescue missions—a time when "Christian charity" required deeds rather than words. One of the most successful charitable organizations working with Chinese prostitutes was the Occidental Board of the San Francisco YWCA. Under the board's auspices, a home was founded in 1881 to shelter Chinese girls rescued from the brothels. The director of the home after 1896 was Donaldina Cameron, the Jane Addams of the West Coast. Although volunteers working with the home often saw themselves as taking up the white man's burden of Kipling's poem, Donaldina Cameron did not approach her work in such a manner.[23]

Under Cameron, rescue work consisted of raiding Chinese brothels where young prostitutes were forced to remain against their will. By the 1890s the home had acquired such a fine reputation for rescue work that prostitutes who wished to be rescued would send word there rather than to the police. For her part, Cameron always took police officers with her; they could be used as protection, to display authority, and to serve as witnesses if it was necessary to appear in court to prove the rescued women had left the brothels by their own choice.[24] Once free of the brothels, the women would live in the home. Some of them were as young as twelve or fourteen, and if they said that they had been kidnapped from their homes in China, every effort was made to reunite them with their families. Others were trained for employment, usually domestic work, and still others married and raised their own families.

Chinese and Latin American prostitutes were unquestionably the most exploited members of the profession, but they were not the only foreign prostitutes to come to San Francisco as indentured servants. On February 2, 1850, the *Alta California* demanded to know why the law had allowed the "sale of three females from Sydney" to raise money for their passage to California. However, it was difficult to sustain sympathy for Australians as long as "Sydney Ducks" were believed responsible for much of the crime and many of the incendiary fires in the city.

The Sydney Ducks had sailed to San Francisco from the British penal colony of Australia. Some had served criminal sentences there and had been released; others may have escaped. But to the xenophobic Californians, all Australians came to be seen as undesirable. Once a few Australians had been caught looting stores during one of the many fires in the city, they were all thought to be a "rowdy and knavish class." In June 1851, after a fifth great fire had devastated the city, the first Committee of Vigilance was founded to patrol against fire and theft. Its primary target was the Sydney Ducks. The crime rate dropped drastically by September, and the vigilantes, having justified their illegal actions through success, disbanded.

The Ducks had made themselves so undesirable that attempts were made to limit the immigration of Australian men. Public pressure did not, of course, become so unreasonable as to turn away Australian women. "Skirted humanity was then [1851] too scarce to deny it entrance on the grounds of badness; so the Sydney sisters were permitted to land." Even when the Vigilance Committee of 1851 met incoming ships in the harbor and refused landing to any Australian man who could not prove he was not an ex-criminal from the penal colony, it did not object to the addition of "four prostitutes from Australia" swelling the ranks of the demimonde.[25]

Prejudiced the early Californians may have been, but until the numbers of women increased sufficiently to allow the American men of San Francisco to be choosey instead of chosen, they could not afford to view foreign women with the same disdain they reserved for foreign men. Irish men might be labeled rowdy and belligerent, but Irish women were the "sparkling daughters of Erin." Hispanic men were sneered at for the shallowness of their "effervescing brilliancy and unsustained dash,"[26] but Californio women, who maintained an aura of haughtiness, were languorous beauties or "beauteous gazelle-eyed maidens."[27] And one group of foreign prostitutes—the French—by displaying cultural pride, demanded and received greater respect, admiration, and fees than even the American prostitutes commanded in the earliest days of the gold rush.

French prostitutes maintained this position throughout the nineteenth century. The most derogatory adjective ascribed to a French prostitute was that she was notorious. Even the harshest critics of "flaunting women of pleasure" acknowledged that the French women "gave ease, taste, and sprightly elegance to the manners of the town."[28]

French prostitutes did not arrive in California in significant numbers until after 1850; then they immediately became the fashion leaders of the demimonde society. "The expensive and fashionable style of dressing among the French ladies . . . greatly encouraged the splendid character of the shops of jewelers, silk merchants, milliners and others whom women chiefly patronize." And it was not only the prostitutes who followed the fashion set by the French women but every "respectable" woman in San Francisco who aspired to elegance and style. It was suggested that the elegance of these women was such that even the miners were encouraged to bathe, shave, and put on clean shirts in order to attract their attention.[29]

The French prostitutes' ability to attract men was obviously the reason so many gambling saloons offered them the highest wages to grace their rooms. One miner described the attraction: "There was a young French woman dealing twenty-one. She was as pretty as a picture. Began betting just to get near her and hear her talk. I lost seventy dollars and she did not notice me any more than she did the rest of the crowd."[30] (He was persistent, however, and eventually persuasive, because Madame Ferrard, the twenty-one dealer, eventually consented not only to notice him but to marry him.)

For the saloon owner, the presence of women in the establishment drew customers; the presence of French women guaranteed crowds. In a description of gambling halls of the early 1850s, Eliza Farnham makes the distinction clear.

> *In one corner [of the hall] a coarse-looking female might preside over a roulette-table, and, perhaps, in the central and crowded part of the room a Spanish or*

Mexican woman would be sitting at monte, with a cigareta in her lips, which she replaced every few moments by a fresh one. In a very few fortunate houses, neat, delicate, and sometimes beautiful French women were every evening to be seen. . . . These houses, to the honor of the coarse crowd be it said, were always filled![31]

Farnham's extensive writings often idealized the place of "respectable" women in frontier society. She even defended the "fallen" women in the west by blaming their fall from "moral purity" on the hardships and temptations that they faced as pioneers. But her physical descriptions of prostitutes are always critical, with the exception of the French. Other women working in gambling halls were coarse, but French women were neat, delicate, and beautiful.

On the surface, such unqualified acclaim is difficult to understand. Even if we could accept the blanket endorsement of the beauty, charm, and grace of *all* French women in San Francisco, it would still not explain their superior position in the institution. Women of all nationalities, including the Latin Americans, at one time or another were given their share of adulation. The French prostitutes who came to San Francisco were not of a particularly refined class in Paris. Albert Benard de Russailh, a Frenchman who arrived in San Francisco in 1851, made it clear in his journal that at home they were "streetwalkers of the cheapest sort." Nevertheless, in San Francisco, for a few minutes of their time, they received a fee one hundred times what they got in Paris. With his own share of cultural chauvinism, Benard found it understandable that men preferred French women; but he was also a little scornful of the prices they were willing to pay.

Americans were irresistibly attracted by their graceful walk, their supple and easy bearing and charming freedom of manners, qualities, after all, only to be found in [Frenchwomen]. If the poor fellows had known what these women had been in Paris, how one could pick them up on the boulevards and have them for almost nothing, they might not have been so free with their offers of five hundred or six hundred dollars a night.[32]

It is clear that the French prostitutes' professional background was no better (and in some cases worse) than other prostitutes in San Francisco. What then is the explanation for their elevated position? In part it was that they had elegance and that they worked to maintain it.

Various chroniclers throughout the century noted that ladylike decorum in the parlor house begot gentlemanly treatment. By cultivating elegance, prostitutes could gain some control over the conditions of their lives. Elegant and refined surroundings also elicited polite behavior on the part of the customers. Furthermore, in the parlor houses, the women were the central attraction, unlike gambling saloons and dance halls, where women were only a lure to men to spend money on drinks and gambling; prostitutes in these settings could not, for example, be offended by coarse language or bawdy songs.

However, French prostitutes had no need of an elegant parlor house. In 1849 and 1850, when the majority of prostitutes worked in gambling saloons or were courtesans, the "fortunate [gambling] houses," as Farnham said, employed French women. When the institution began to separate into distinct divisions and to develop a corresponding hierarchy, the French prostitutes continued to be the elite in both social position and income, whatever the setting.

By 1856, although there were all-French parlor houses and American parlor houses that employed French women, many French women worked on their own, as prostitutes did in 1849 and 1850, but without damaging their elite status in the changing world of the institution. They continued to work in gambling saloons, dealing cards, selling cigars, or singing, and took their customers to their own apartments in boarding houses or hotels, where "their names and reception hours" were written on their doors. Non-French prostitutes in similar conditions were subject to derogatory references in the daily press, but being French continued to be sufficient reason for being referred to with polite euphemisms, such as the "charming demoiselles of France."[33]

The unique position of the French prostitute was based undoubtedly on two intangible factors—the self-image of the French and the world's admiration of everything French. Benard was quite complacent about the superiority of French culture in multicultural San Francisco. Arriving in 1851, he moved with relief into a French hotel where he felt comfortable, despite the fact that the furnishings of the room consisted of four mattresses on the floor. Commercial Street (called Frenchtown) was the most interesting thoroughfare in town, according to Benard, with its "shops right out on the pavement . . . making it a regular market place."[34]

Also on Commercial Street were the French gambling saloons, where only French games were played. Benard declared that "gambling here is organized robbery"; cards were stacked, wheels were fixed, and "God help the man who falls victim." Without acknowledging any contradiction, he made an exception of the French saloons: "*Of course,* these places are fair but the banker has so much advantage that the player" still cannot win. He accepted as natural that French prostitutes were preferred, just as he reported that, at public dances, Frenchwomen "*of course* . . . dance with more grace and vivre" than Americans, who were stiff, and Mexicans, who were languorous.[35] Benard's ethnocentricity was most blatant when it came to the theater. French plays were not always good, but they were "the only civilized distraction in [the] new city." As theater critic for a French journal, he attended both American and French productions. Though he preferred the American theater for its physical comfort, he had a great many compliments for the French troupes that performed in the French theater. He gave them good reviews for bad performances, seemingly for no other reason than that they were French and that their efforts to bring civilization to people on the verge of reverting to "barbarism" had to be encouraged. For the women directors he had nothing but praise. After only two years in California, he boasted, they owned the building, lot, and scenery. The fact that they had "not earned all their money in the theater" was beside the point. If there were "certain wealthy patrons of the arts in the background," it was only to be expected. They were, after all, Frenchwomen.[36]

Benard's attitude was not unique. The French assumed that French culture was superior. The *Annals* in 1854 reported that the French were less willing to adopt American thoughts and fashions than other nationalities and were uninterested in learning English. It is reasonable to suppose that the *last* concessions the French would have made to their new environment would be to give up their most universally admired cultural traits—language, fashion, and ideas. The writings, actions, and expectations of French immigrants, including the prostitutes, seemed to suggest that French culture was superior and San Francisco was fortunate to have such a civilizing influence on its heterogeneous society.[37]

All this helps explain the exalted position of French prostitutes. In fashion, France was the undisputed leader, and in San Francisco the French prostitute set the style in dress for all women. To use French words to describe prostitutes removed the derogatory connotations—*filles de pavé* and *demoiselles* were the standard newspaper terms in 1849 and 1850. Such phrases could even be used in the presence of "respectable" ladies, when terms like *whore* and *harlot* were shocking and vulgar. More common French terms, like *courtesan* and *demimonde,* had already become part of the English language. French art, music, and literature were also admired and, combined with its romantic history of courts of love, chivalry, and the exploits of kings and their mistresses, endowed French women with a sensuality that in other nationalities would have been associated with lewdness and debauchery.

Execution of James P. Casey and Charles Cora.

Warner's opened in 1856 and closed with the owner's death in 1897. The specialty of the house was boiling whiskey, gin, and cloves. Warner liked spiders and never brushed away one of their webs. The Saloon's interior was festooned with cob-

webs. Visible behind the cobwebs on the wall were paintings of naked women. In addition, cages of monkeys, parrots, and other small animals along with carved walrus tusks "graced" the decor.

San Francisco in 1849. Drawing by Henry Firks.

S.H.WILLIAMS & CO.

San Francisco in 1856, showing the phenomenal growth that had taken place in just seven years (despite the fact that the city was nearly destroyed by five major fires as well as countless smaller conflagrations).

FORD'S
EAN GALLERY
NG WARE HOUSE
RTION BET. WASHINGTON & SACRAMENTO STS. 1856.
FARDON.

Maguire's Opera House on Washington Street. Tom Maguire purchased the original structure and enlarged it to a three-story building. Actress Adah Isaacs Menken performed "Mazeppa" at Maguire's in 1863 and became the toast of the West, and shortly after of two continents, with the famous horseback-riding scene.

V. WORKING WOMEN

In American society, prostitution has never been a respectable form of employment. Even in the San Francisco of 1849 and 1850, prostitutes maintained their respectable status *in spite of* their profession, not because they were professionals. During the second half of the nineteenth century, society was publicly moral. A "fallen woman," the poets and novelists of the period reminded their readers, was "once a child with a mother—was once innocent and pure." Their advice was to have compassion and sympathy for the woman who was "lost," but there was no suggestion that she be reinstated in respectable society.[1]

That women who became prostitutes would be "condemned . . . by social decree to banishment" was a well-known fact of life and suggests why many nonprofessionals would have been reluctant to accept the fact that they were prostitutes. How much eventual acceptance of professional status was a defiance of society's dictates cannot be measured. One analyst of nineteenth-century prostitution speculated that, "debarred from normal association with right-minded people . . . they come at last to adopt the standards and live the life of the class to which society condemns them."[2]

The belief that prostitutes were irretrievably lost to respectability was widely held, but in San Francisco it was not rigidly adhered to. Prostitutes there married into all classes of society.[3] Some went into other businesses. The position retired prostitutes held in society, however, usually depended on their ability to hide their earlier calling. One well-known example was Mary Ellen Pleasant, whose public reputation was that of a housekeeper but who had in her colorful career in San Francisco been "kept" by a number of men, had run or owned elegant brothels and assignation houses, and had acted as a marriage broker for some of the women who had worked for her in her parlor houses. Despite her easy financial success, she was careful to maintain a reputation for respectability during and following her involvement with prostitution. The facade of respectability maintained by Mary Ellen Pleasant and others like her helped to sustain the belief that once a woman was known to be a prostitute there was no turning back.[4]

The difficulty of identifying as a prostitute a woman who maintained her nonprofessional image must have been a welcome safeguard for women who did not want to face the realities of their situation. A woman who was the mistress of one man at a time, for example, was not condemned as a prostitute. The line between mistress and prostitute, however, was a fine one. By nineteenth-century usage and definition, a prostitute was any woman who offered her body for "base gain." According to this definition, a prostitute could be a mistress—though not all mistresses were prostitutes. Only in the definition of mistress do we find the word love mentioned; only in the practice of performing a sex act for financial gain rather than love is the prostitute separated from the paramour or mistress. It may be supposed, therefore, that some women, unable to accept the stigma of the term *prostitute,* rationalized their situation by declaring affection for the men who supported them.

Why then did women who would feel obliged to rationalize or justify their action become prostitutes at all? The obvious reason was economic necessity. Women in the nineteenth century who had to support themselves found that the opportunities to do so were limited. In the West, not even the low wages of factory employment were available.[5] The large eastern-style factories employing women did not develop in San Francisco until after the 1869 completion of the transcontinental railroad. Even then, development was slow; the opening up of jobs to women was even slower. In

1870, the first year women were found in the statistics of industrial employees in San Francisco, only five manufacturers hired women. In 1885, that number had increased to thirteen—but there were eighty-eight industrial categories in the city at the time.[6]

During the twenty years following the discovery of gold, women's choices remained limited. *The Hesperian* pointed out in a series of articles on "Employment for Women" in 1858: "there is no room for women [in the work force]; the avenues where she may labor are *few*, and at best *undesirable*. . . . When we mention school-teaching and keeping boarders, we have covered the entire ground upon which woman may labor for her daily bread."[7]

Mrs. F. H. Day, publisher of *The Hesperian*, was referring to respectable occupations for middle-class women who had never been faced with the necessity of laboring for their daily bread. Poor women might earn miserable wages as laundresses or domestic servants. No matter what their class, and despite any mitigating circumstances, women lost caste when they had to work. It was Day's contention that if women, barred from business and labor, and dependent upon men for support, were forced to provide for themselves, then it was the men who should suffer the loss of respect, not the women.[8]

This article was neither the first nor the last to appear in the *Hesperian* dealing with employment opportunities for women; all emphasized the continuing difficulty women had in supporting themselves in San Francisco. In one of the first issues of the journal, Day devoted a full column to admonishing women to improve themselves so as to deserve the respect they had as American women. Both upper-class and working women were capable of being more useful to society—if they had the opportunity. Finally, in the last paragraph of the column, she placed the blame where she felt it belonged. Women could not improve their condition as long as "that [job] which no man of spirit will touch is always good enough for woman . . . employments are vouchsafed; and these prices [wages] are paid by *men*, and among *men*—men who would have the women of this country believe that they have a hearty desire to promote the welfare the comfort and the goodness of Women! God forgive them!"[9]

Men, with their "hearty desire to promote . . . the goodness of Women," were the crux of the problem for all working women, prostitutes and nonprostitutes alike. Women like Day and Farnham placed the blame on the fact that one set of rules of conduct was maintained for women and another for men. The economic double standard was strong in nineteenth-century America, and it appeared to be there to stay. Women were told by editors like James King of the *Evening Bulletin* (January 25 and 26, 1856), that it was deplorable for them to have an occupation. It was their duty, he reminded women, to be in the home "refining society." When a reader asked him what women should do if they had to earn a living, he admitted that that was a problem he had never considered, and he "must think about it."

Those women who waited for King to "think about it" were disappointed—he never referred to the matter again. In the meantime, they were probably searching for employment. In 1849, 1850, and 1851, a lucrative choice might have been washerwoman. By 1852, though, there were enough washerwomen and Chinese laundries to force the price from eight dollars down to five dollars for a dozen pieces. Laundry work was demeaning and, after 1851, no longer financially rewarding. It involved another difficulty as well: water was always in short supply in San Francisco and the one convenient place for washing large amounts of clothing, "washerwoman's lagoon," was in the area of Little Chile, never a safe section of the city.[10]

By 1855, the Chinese laundries had a relatively secure monopoly on the laundry business, but private homes, though still scarce, were becoming more numerous in San Francisco, so that it was possible for a woman to find work as a servant for fifty to seventy-five dollars per month. Although these were pretty substantial wages for the period, they came nowhere near meeting the cost for a woman with children to live in San Francisco in an inflationary time. The minimum rent for one room was $20 a month, a cord of wood cost $15, meat was 37¢ a pound, eggs $1.25 a dozen, and milk 25¢ a quart.[11]

After 1854, low-paid jobs were available in sewing, cooking, and clerking, when stores catering to women opened in the city. Sewing and cooking required a certain degree of skill, as well as competition with men. Although fine sewing work, like laces and silks, was still women's work, with the invention of the sewing machine in 1846 men were more commonly hired in factories that produced inexpensive everyday garments. Woolen mills producing ready-made clothing were among the first factories to open in San Francisco, but women were not considered capable of running the machines. Cooking was another possibility, but the only place women were preferred over men as cooks was in the boarding houses. In most cases, however, the wives of the owners did the cooking.[12]

Another area of employment open to women in the East was that of clerk. But out of an estimated seven thousand women in San Francisco in 1852, only two were listed as store employees. It is not clear whether the two women working in stores were single employed women or were working for a father, brother, or husband. The numerous reminiscences of the early pioneers made no mention of female clerks in the establishments of San Francisco merchants. Since women were still scarce enough to be referred to in memoirs whenever they were encountered, this omission is significant.[13]

Further evidence is found in the daily newspapers, again by omission. In 1849 and 1850, and to a lesser degree throughout the decade of the 1850s, most of the space in newspapers was devoted to advertisements—or cards, as they were called. Merchants often listed, item by item, new shipments in stock. There were advertisements for the sale of property, mining equipment, livestock, boots, and other items, but, until late 1853 and 1854, there were none written to appeal to women. There were no family grocery stores before this time, no female emporiums, no establishments that might be expected to hire female clerks to wait on customers.[14]

In the East, the position of female clerk developed only when "off the rack" (mass produced) clothing became as reasonably priced as homemade garments. It was generally considered indelicate to have male clerks wait on women customers in such establishments.[15] By 1860 in San Francisco, a growing number of businesses were devoted to women's clothes, but the lack of female clerks prompted a poem entitled "Woman's Sphere," which appeared in the *Hesperian* (pp. 309–10) in March 1860 under the pen name *Phosphor:*

When God conceived the wondrous plan
  And wrought the great creation,
To woman-kind, as well as man,
  There was assigned a station.

Yet rumor, with her thousand tongues,
  Has told us many a story
Of woman's rights and woman's wrongs,
  More to man's shame than glory.

To Frisco I resolved to go
  And learn her true position;
To find if all they said was so,
  About her sad condition.

. . . .

I wandered on, and entered next
  A *first-class* bonnet-store:
Here too a pair of striped pants
  Was stationed at the door.

And pale-faced girls, with care-worn brows,
  Grown prematurely old,
Were for a pittance making up
  The goods their brothers sold.

. . . .

Next came a "Ladies' Clothing Store";
  Here hoops—the grand extension—
And other little nameless things
  I wouldn't like to mention,

Were held to view by clerks well skilled
  To please a lady's eye;
One twirled his mustache while he praised
  The goods I came to buy.

"If men will deal in ladies' gear,
  Why, let them not complain,
Though women doff the petticoat
  And don coat, pants, and cane.

"Nor let them wonder when they hear
  'T is held in contemplation
To give them—each and every one—
  A *pressing* invitation—

"Assistance, if they like, to don
  The garments of the ladies;
Show to the world their chosen sphere,
  And show, too, what their trade is."

The situation did not improve in the 1860s for women seeking employment in any field within their "sphere." There was a slight recession in the labor market in the early 1860s, and men were hired for the few jobs open to women. As salaries for teachers improved on the frontier, more men than women were hired for those positions. Male Chinese servants were hired before white female servants because they worked for less.[16] The situation was so acute by 1860 that Day warned working women that if they lost the jobs they held to men, they would "have but one choice . . . starvation or moral degradation."

When women like Day or Isabelle Saxon, a British visitor to San Francisco in 1861, referred to "moral degradation," they were not speaking exclusively of prostitution, but also work in beer parlors, gambling saloons, and barrooms.[17]

Saxon was especially concerned that economic necessity would lead women into moral danger. In her memoirs of life in San Francisco, she relates story after story of girls as well as widowed or deserted mothers with young children forced to take employment in bars or on the stage. The result appeared to Saxon, as well as to other writers of the period, as inevitable. In the saloons,

> *customers . . . are served by attractive-looking girls, who are unfortunately too often of degraded morals. What better could be hoped of females tempted by poverty to accept such places, exposed, too, to the necessity of often accepting liquor from the customer . . . in order to gratify him, for the purpose of pleasing the employer by pleasing the customer, or else hazarding the retention of the situation!*[18]

It was undoubtedly because of the lack of alternatives for economic survival that some women first turned to nonprofessional prostitution. There were, for example, the servants who accepted gifts of money from a "gentleman friend" because their wages were not sufficient to "keep soul and body together." The waiter girls who took occasional customers to their rooms for additional income—or possibly to keep their jobs—were also part of the nonprofessional strata. Some of these took the long step and became professionals.[19]

Recruitment into the professional ranks was not limited to women who became prostitutes out of extreme economic need. The general excitement of the period and the unusual position women held as a result of their scarcity led many to act in ways they would not have contemplated before coming to San Francisco. Married as well as single women met lovers in the numerous assignation houses in the city. This phenomenon was not exclusive to San Francisco, but contemporary writers reported that in this city the practice was more widespread than elsewhere: "Numbers of the sex have fallen very readily into the evil ways of the place. Perhaps the more 'lovely' they were, the more readily they 'stooped to folly.' It is difficult for any woman, however pure, to preserve an unblemished reputation in a community like San Francisco."[20]

Observers like Sarah Royce, who viewed those who "stooped to folly" without sympathy, found the moral decline of formerly respectable women more distressing than acknowledged prostitutes. According to Royce, such women were weak and vain; they held their "convictions too lightly; and as they came to feel the force of unwonted excitement and the pressure of unexpected temptation, they too often yielded." The temptations were adulation and expensive presents, and Royce "blushed to discover" that even women with husbands were jealous of each other's presents and admiration and joined the competition for male attention.[21]

Royce dwelt primarily on the downfall of married women. They let themselves be led astray, she believed, by "weak vanity," which led them to desert husbands and children. Their degradation was eventually complete when they were in turn deserted by their lovers. Royce seldom divided the blame between men and women. "There were but few ladies" there, anyway, and if they yielded to temptation "there must have been sad corruption somewhere" in their character to start with.[22]

Not all observers were as harsh as Royce, or as willing to

accept the view that only women could set the moral standards of society. Bancroft, for example, did not believe that it was the lack of respectable women in California that determined the low morals of the new state, because women lived in the moral atmosphere men created for them. If, therefore, they had been in the migration of 1849, "it is probable that as a whole, and to a certain extent, they would have fallen into excess [gambling, drinking, loose morals] themselves, instead of withholding their companions entirely from them."[23]

Although he did not always succeed in persuading others, Bancroft recognized and rejected the double standard that governed views of contemporary men and women. To him, women were no more immune to their environment and associates than men. If the lack of social restraints explained the immoral actions of men, then the same had to be true for the "weaker" sex. "To live in purity," he claimed, "woman must have the sympathy of those around her; thousands in California have fallen simply from the fact that men had no faith in them."[24]

Eliza Farnham wrote in similar terms.

> *It is so hard to natures, that have not more than common strength, to live uprightly and purely, when they feel that there is no sympathy with their life, in those who surround them—and, still worse, no faith. To be always doubted is, to the integrity of common minds, to be as the stone under the fountain that never ceases dropping.*[25]

Both writers were offering explanations for those women who drifted into prostitution because of the climate of excitement in San Francisco. Farnham, however, was not merely an apologist for these women. Men who complained about the morals of California women, she observed, were the same ones "making themselves familiar with the worst side of our social life rather than the best" and were ignoring the fact that they had produced the worst side. "Dereliction from moral purity" was unfortunate, she admitted, but "there is nothing from which we need shrink, in the comparison of our sex in California, with the sterner and more boastful one."[26]

Eliza Farnham and Sarah Royce were contemporaries.

Both were educated migrants from the East Coast who were part of San Francisco society in 1850 and 1851. Yet Royce accepted woman's traditional role, was herself morally strong, and found no excuse for those who deviated from what she perceived to be proper conduct. She endured the hardships of the overland journey with her husband and child, and followed him from mining camps to San Francisco and back again while he tried to make his fortune through various business enterprises. Despite the unconventional atmosphere of the frontier, she remained a conventional wife. She was dependent upon her husband for support and direction and, quite simply, avoided personal contact with anyone who did not meet her standards.[27]

Farnham, like Royce, found very little to attract her in frontier social life, but her objections were based on inferior intellectual companions rather than on inferior moral companions. A widow, Farnham was not dependent on a husband. She journeyed to California with her children to straighten out the financial problems left by her husband's untimely death there. When she discovered that the farm he left her in Santa Cruz could not sustain them, she supplemented her income by writing and giving lectures. There is no suggestion that Farnham questioned her own moral strength, but because she was responsible not only for her own support and that of her children, as well as occasional indigent friends, she was more tolerant than most people toward women who were forced to work.[28]

Farnham constantly pointed out the inconsistency of the public's condemnation of prostitutes. As a young woman, she recognized the double moral standard when a *gentleman* she had expected to marry asked her instead to be his mistress. Even the young Eliza was strong-minded. Her reaction was anger:

> *for I had . . . gathered sufficient knowledge of social law, to understand that a man might, without disgrace, do deeds, whose very shadow, falling upon the fame of a woman, would send her shivering to ruin. I had learned that my sex, always reckoned the weakest, always expected to trust to the protective power and strength of man, was entitled to do so only while it was faultless;*

> *but I did not know—how could I?—that, being so, in all matters of social purity, a woman was yet lawful game, which a man might hunt without censure, and lure to destruction, without sacrificing, in any degree, his pretentions to rank as a gentleman.*[29]

The kind of proposition that had so angered Eliza Farnham led some San Francisco women to become prostitutes. Mistresses had at their disposal numerous facilities that allowed them to meet their lovers with minimal fear of detection. There were rooms in boarding houses that were houses of assignation, which either the man or the woman could rent for an afternoon or an evening. The managers of these establishments were discreet, carefully preserving the identities of their clientele, who were publicly respectable.[30]

Equally popular with couples meeting clandestinely were the public resorts and restaurants that offered "private rooms for supper open all night." In all such establishments, "the object of the proprietor [was] to preserve secrecy."[31] Until these women were ready to accept the fact that they were prostituting, anonymity and the illusion of respectability were their primary concerns.

One other group of prostitutes also escaped society's scorn; these were the victims of the white-slave traffic, whom society viewed in much the same way as Chinese prostitutes. These prostitutes were usually between thirteen and seventeen years of age and were clearly victims of a crime rather than participants in vice. Widespread concern over the white-slave trade did not manifest itself until the 1880s, but reformers claimed it had been prevalent in San Francisco since the early 1850s. From the quantity of written material dealing with involuntary prostitution (primarily after the 1880s), it would appear that society was almost relieved to be able to discuss the topic on some respectable level. Once the subject of prostitution was broached, attempts were made to examine and answer all questions raised about the problem of the enslavement into prostitution of innocent girls.[32]

In San Francisco, as in most major cities in the United States, the job of aiding the victims of forced prostitution and of making the public aware of the problem was carried on by church groups, mission workers, and social reformers in the

1880s. Their activities included removing from brothels any minors being kept there against their will or forced to work in the establishment. Rescue workers would usually wait for a request for help, then enter the brothel and walk out with the girl who had contacted them. In other instances, if they knew a particular house specialized in girls, they would invade it in the company of a policeman and ask if any of the girls there wanted to leave with them. The rescue and all other aspects of the girls' experiences were explained to the public by the rescue workers. Rehabilitation methods, such as training in domestic work or sewing, were carefully drawn to educate the public and to gain public support for the agency.[33]

All studies describe the same methods of recruitment: seduction or force employed by professional procurers. Sometimes a presentable man would strike up an acquaintance with a girl and court her assiduously until she agreed to spend the night with him in a hotel. If the girl were strictly raised, he might be forced to promise marriage or even to go through a mock marriage ceremony, with an accomplice acting as minister. The girl would wake in the morning to find that her "husband" had abandoned her and that the "hotel" was actually a brothel. A bawd would lock her in the room until she agreed to work as a prostitute. If she was difficult to persuade, she would be drugged and, in some cases, raped, until her spirit was broken and she accepted the inevitable—prostitution.[34]

The most successful method of forcing working-class girls into prostitution was through employment agencies. The agency would advertise in the East, offering high pay and travel expenses for girls wanted as domestic workers in the West. Once they arrived in San Francisco or Sacramento, the girls found themselves locked inside brothels for the "breaking-in" process—which might include drugs, rape, or confinement—until they were convinced there was "no other life open to them [except] prostitution after such an experience, and that their relatives [would] not take them back." Convincing girls that a return to society and family, once they had yielded to seduction, was closed to them was also an important element in the "training."[35]

Writers on white slavery described the girls with dramatic innuendo: Mary Edholm describes a brothel in which eight to ten girls dressed in schoolgirl garb waited for customers. "If someone had taken a knife and drawn it across the throat of every one and left her weltering in her blood upon that splendid carpet it would not have been one ten-thousandth so bad as what she was waiting for."[36] The "fate worse than death" theme was useful to reformers in urging instruction for girls in the pitfalls of seduction. It also gave them a platform from which to preach better religious training and better wages for working girls, both popular reform goals in the 1880s. At the same time, reformers could entreat society to accept the victims back into the fold and offer them rehabilitation.[37]

The theme of rehabilitation was evidence of the change in society's view by the 1880s. In the earlier decades of the Victorian era, the idea of accepting a "fallen woman" back into respectable society was unthinkable, unless the woman remained true to the Victorian code of public conformity, and had kept her shame secret. To publicly advocate not only forgiveness but the reestablishment of respectability mandated a new approach to the question of fallen women. This the nineteenth-century rescue workers attempted to accomplish, in their literature, explaining forced prostitution and offering solutions. Their purpose was to rouse public sympathy and draw financial support and volunteer workers. This literature suggests that girls in middle-class homes were so sheltered and protected that in their naiveté they fell victim to the traffic in girls. The literature does not explain how such overly protected girls could clandestinely meet professional procurers. It is even harder to accept that working girls would have walked into a common brothel believing it to be a respectable home where they might be hired as a servant.[38]

The image of a young, innocent, naive, and impoverished victim undoubtedly had some basis in fact; both hearsay evidence and firsthand reports were overwhelming. Too overwhelming—the stereotype was repeated continually throughout the late nineteenth and early twentieth century, seldom varying in any of the main particulars. For this reason, it is difficult to accept without qualification the massive data on white slavery.

What the literature failed to provide was a full picture

of the prostitute's view of her life and of the conditions of her work. She was always protrayed as passive. Everything happened *to* her: she was procured; she was prostituted; she was rescued; she was rehabilitated. The only time the prostitute was recognized as a thinking, functioning person was when she either refused to be rescued or voluntarily returned to prostitution after being rescued. These were the actions of a real person, however much it might be pointed out that she had become addicted to drugs, alcohol, or debauchery by others.[39] As a victim she had no personality: she manifested no trace of intelligence, wit, ambition, survival instinct, virtue, or vice.

We might, however, find a clue to how they felt about their situation from the biographies and memoirs of twentieth-century madams and prostitutes. Some of these at age fourteen or fifteen were "lured" by a professional procurer into prostitution, but persuasion and the enticements of expensive presents and high wages were the deciding factors, not force. Other women worked or lived in hotels and boarding houses, where they associated with prostitutes who persuaded them to take advantage of the easy money to be made. There were those who claimed the procurer had gotten them drunk and that they woke to discover that they had been raped. Their reaction may have been shock, anger, or resignation, but the decision they made, in the end, to accept prostitution, was a reasoned one made by an identifiable person.[40]

Most writers and reformers of the time also believed that the white-slave trade was nationally and even internationally organized. At the culmination of the panic (which led to the Mann Act of 1910), international congresses were held to find solutions to the problem. No evidence of any large-scale organization dealing in traffic in women was found by any of the investigating committees. The bulk of the evidence supports the contention that most women were recruited or lured into the ranks of prostitution by offers of wealth, pleasure, or an easy life.[41]

To question the stereotype of white-slavery victims is not to deny their existence; young women were constantly procured to work in the brothels and cribs of the Barbary Coast and of most major cities in the country. Modern studies as well as contemporary accounts (despite their hysterical tone) are ample evidence that such traffic in women took place. The most likely victims were unattached young immigrant women, whose disappearance would raise no outcry from their families, or young factory workers who might easily be convinced that five dollars or more a night was preferable to five dollars a week and being "friendly" with the boss. Some women were, at least in the beginning, recruited into this employment by involuntary means.

Beyond that, it is difficult to accept that these women had to be continually coerced to prostitute. Such recalcitrant employees would have been more trouble than they were worth. Might they not have reported their coercion to a customer? Did all the men who paid for a prostitute ignore pleas for help? Could they fail to notice a partner too drugged to be coherent? Not only were such questions never answered—they were never asked. Such omissions cast doubt on the veracity of the accounts used by reform and rescue workers to make their case.[42] Explaining the economic inducements to remain in prostitution would have been detrimental to their cause.

Prostitutes who made the choice to be in or stay in the profession eventually moved into the professional hierarchy, a transition that did not necessarily improve their condition. After the 1850s, downward was more prevalent than upward mobility, according to San Francisco chroniclers. The admiration and respect that prostitutes experienced in 1850 declined continually throughout the rest of the century. Suicides by alleged prostitutes averaged some eight to ten per year.[43] Despite the opportunity for high financial rewards, prostitution was a harsh, taxing life; very few women who entered the profession failed to realize that fact. Nevertheless, the choice is not difficult to understand when one looks at the options women had available to them.

VI. ON THE FRINGE: CORRUPTION AND REFORM

An examination of the business enterprises and occupations that profited from prostitution suggests why the institution is called the "oldest profession in the world." If financial rewards were limited only to prostitutes, reformers in San Francisco (or anywhere else) might have found it easier to get legislation against women and houses of ill fame passed and enforced. Such was not the case. The profits from prostitution accrued to a wide sector of society.

There has always been a tendency to attribute the profits from prostitution only to the individual prostitute; in reality, the women worked in the most insecure part of the business. They were the ones subject to disease, harassment, arrest, competition, and unemployment. On the other hand, profits for those on the fringe relied on large numbers of prostitutes and a constant turnover in their ranks.

In cities like San Francisco with large and flourishing red-light districts, many people made money directly or indirectly from prostitutes. For some, such as mantua makers (dress designers), doctors, liquor salesmen, and theater managers, the trade represented a substantial but only partial portion of their income. Others, such as cadets (pimps), madams, brothel owners, and procurers, relied solely on the continuation of the institution to make a living. A third group, consisting of police, judges, and other municipal officials, received gratuities from prostitutes not to perform their duties.

The list can be expanded indefinitely according to the year, the goods or services provided, and the individual prostitute's social class. In the earliest days of San Francisco, for example, merchants selling such luxury items as elegant furniture and hangings or delicacies were patronized primarily by prostitutes. Only prostitutes and parlor-house madams had the finances, the inclination, and the incentive to be concerned with the elegance and luxury of their dwellings.[1]

As the city stabilized, men turned from mining and speculation to their traditional occupations. Carriage makers, carpenters, and bricklayers did a thriving business among the demimonde. By the 1850s, jewelers, silk merchants, shoemakers, and milliners capitalized on the influence of the French prostitutes by opening expensive and fashionable shops of "splendid character." Employment opportunities grew for musicians, florists, and servants because of the patronage of prostitutes.[2] Most San Franciscans lived in hotels and boarding houses, so houses of prostitution were the main customers for luxury items for the home.

The same was true for merchants who sold clothing and jewelry for women.[3] Prostitutes were the most visible women in San Francisco even in the mid-1850s, when they were surpassed in number by respectable women. They were not shy about "sweeping along" in their fashionable gowns, "apparently proud of being recognized as one of frail character." Public display of the latest fashions in dress and expensive gems was a valuable source of advertising for the merchant or designer.[4] And though "In Eastern cities the prostitute tried to imitate in manner and dress the fashionable respectable ladies . . . in San Francisco the rule was reversed—the latter copying the former."[5]

Less public but just as dependent on prostitution were the abortionists, who relied on word-of-mouth advertising. Physicians who specialized in the dreaded occupational diseases of prostitution were more open. Whether their patients were prostitutes or their customers was unclear, but their literature carried such titles as "Cure for Youthful Indiscretions," "Young Men, Take Warning," and "Let the Afflicted Read."[6]

In California from the earliest days of the gold rush doctors composed a disproportionately high percentage of the population. An 1850 account lists twenty-nine doctors in the small mining town of Rich Bar. The 1860 census reports 1,122 physicians and 16 surgeons in California. In the nineteenth century, it was a common practice for a man to study, or read, medicine with a practicing physician rather than attend medical school. No one knows how many claiming the title of doctor had even read medicine, but the *San Francisco News Letter* in 1876 kept an updated list of approximately 300 doctors in San Francisco who had no medical certificate or diploma.[7] In the eighteenth, nineteenth, and twentieth centuries, madams of the better-class brothels and parlor houses kept doctors on retainer to regularly examine and treat their employees.[8]

The link between prostitution and the theater was very close as well. Many actresses were part-time prostitutes who entertained male theatergoers in the "green room" (the reception room) following a performance. The popularity of the green room caused the "respectable" to view actresses with suspicion.[9] Prostitutes as customers were also an economic necessity to the theaters' business. From the first performance of *Jeems Pipes* in 1849, theatergoing was a favorite pastime of San Franciscans. A full house was assured provided the performers lived up to the standards of the city's discriminating clientele.[10]

During the decade of the 1850s, at least, San Francisco prostitutes were not relegated to a separate place in the theater. Belle Cora's presence in the "respectable" section of the audience in 1855 is well documented. In the East, common prostitutes occupied the third tier of seats, where they met their customers. "The third tier dictated the very design of the theater building, was at the foundation of theatrical economics, and was largely responsible for the reputation, and consequently the clientele, of the nineteenth-century theater."[11] Once the Barbary Coast was established San Francisco had its share of common prostitutes, and when Wade's Opera House was built in 1876—the largest in the city, the third largest in the country, and advertised as rivaling the finest theater in the country—it contained a third tier.[12]

Whether Wade's included a third tier to accommodate prostitutes and to assure itself the largest possible clientele is speculative. Theater managers seldom admitted to courting patronage among the demimonde. By the 1870s, the undesirable elements in the audiences at San Francisco theaters drew some public attention, however. In 1875, the Bella Union Theater's management, in an attempt to change its unsavory reputation and become a "respectable" theater, assured customers that there would be "no indecent conduct permitted either on the stage or in the audience." The Union was not large enough for a third tier, but like most San Francisco theaters it offered private stalls (which could be completely curtained off) for fifty-five dollars, while pit and box seats went for three and five dollars, respectively.[13]

Theater owners, doctors, jewelers, and dressmakers were only some of the legitimate business and professional people to profit from prostitution. The financial impact of prostitution on San Francisco was at least one reason for the notoriously lax enforcement of anti-vice laws. Ordinances against prostitution were enforced primarily among Chinese and Latin American women—precisely those who, as individuals, had the least financial impact on the city's private sector. The Chinese were clannish and generally patronized professionals and merchants of their own race, and consequently their economic impact was less obvious. Latin American prostitutes, at the bottom of the hierarchy, were neither fashion setters nor residents of parlor houses or brothels. While the economic benefit to the business community was only one factor affecting enforcement of anti-vice ordinances, it helps to explain the absence of any broad-based support for reform movements.

In 1906, evidence gathered in bribery trials against municipal authorities in San Francisco showed that houses of prostitution paid large sums of money to the mayor, the city "boss," the board of supervisors, and various licensing commissioners to assure their continued existence.[14] (By then, bribery had been perfected by over fifty years of practice. In 1849, Charles Howe, a gold seeker from the East Coast, was recruited off the street to serve on one of the first juries assembled in the city. While the jury deliberated, a bag of gold dust was passed through a hole in the fence of the courthouse yard where the jury was sequestered. Howe divided the gold among the six jurors for finding in favor of the plaintiff. As jury foreman, he kept the larger portion for himself.)[15]

By the turn of the century bribery was less crude and took the guise of consultants' fees or legal retainers, but in the period between 1849 and 1906, methods ranged from payoffs to offers of favored treatment in brothels or parlor houses, especially for judges. A prostitute appearing before Judge Tilford in 1850 charged one of her customers with assault and battery. The July 6 *California Courier* acknowledged the Judge to be "not only humane, but *partial* to the daughters of 'old mother Eve,' and would advise all Ladies who suffer wrongs, to apply at the Recorder's Court for redress; they will be sure to get it."

Even more notorious for their partiality toward the daughters of old mother Eve were judges Murray and McGowan, who were well known for keeping "lewd women as companions" and seldom convicted any in their court.[16] Edward (Ned) McGowan's involvement with "numerous and costly cyprians," and his habit of residing for long periods at parlor houses like Madam Du Bon Court's, eventually turned a usually complacent public against him. His association with James Casey, the noted gambler who shot the editor of the *Evening Bulletin* in 1856, forced McGowan to flee San Francisco to escape the "court," if not the rope, of the Vigilance Committee. He sought refuge and aid from women like the French prostitute Lenny, who wrote to him during his exile in Sacramento inviting him to visit her.[17]

By the 1860s there were few judges like McGowan left. The number of Anglo prostitutes arrested or convicted was still small, but where the *California Courier* in 1850 had noted favored treatment for the "fair but frail," the *California Police Gazette* on April 26, 1862, noted a reversal of that practice, objecting to the meager twenty-five dollar fine against one James Dobson for "Assault on a Noted Cyprian." Although Lizzie Oliver, "a well known courtesan . . . occupying the mansion of the late notorious Belle Cora" had refused to admit Dobson to the house, he had forced his way in, declaring "neither doors nor wh——s could keep him out." The *Gazette* protested: "Be these women what they may, they are, nevertheless entitled to protection against a set of loafers who, in their drunken sprees, force themselves into their houses."

Lizzie undoubtedly had taken care to pay the police in her neighborhood to protect her from arrest. The practice was common. By the 1870s there was even competition among the police for assignment to the lucrative Barbary Coast or Chinese section of town, where gratuities were not only expected but counted on to help toward an early retirement. Methods of payoffs might have been handled more subtly than they were when Howe received his bribe, but there was little attempt to be more secretive.[18]

On November 18, 1865, the *Gazette* did not even bother to add one of its frequent editorial comments on the lack of conviction of one Mrs. Brown, whose neighbors had complained about the number of visitors to her house. The fact that the policeman on the beat admitted that Mrs. Brown had paid him not to arrest her for keeping a house was insufficient evidence for the judge. Also, every witness brought forward to testify that Number Ten Stockton Place was a house of prostitution refused to answer when asked if he had been "on or into bed" with Mrs. Brown, "because he might tend to incriminate or degrade himself." The question itself raised doubts about the seriousness of the prosecutor's intentions. By admitting their presence, the witnesses would have been subject to prosecution as visitors to a house of ill fame, and there was no report of immunity being offered.

Throughout the remainder of the century, San Francisco newspapers commented, with changing degrees of scorn and indignation, on the practice of police payoffs by prostitutes. These criticisms, however, had little effect. In 1876, payoffs were still made openly enough for Benjamin E. Lloyd to comment that prostitution was hard to control when "in these days of official corruption, it does not take many glittering coins to dazzle the eyes of the ordinary policeman so much as to obscure his vision, when he turns his gaze in the direction of dens of vice and infamy."[19]

If by magic reformers could have closed "the dens of vice and infamy" and abolished prostitution, the impact on the economic life of San Francisco would have been severe. Nevertheless, though they would have suffered a significant drop in income, some of those on the fringe of prostitution were not wholly dependent upon prostitution. Such was not the case for others.

The people closest to the institution—madams, bawds,

procurers, and cadets—were often the link between the individual prostitute and the business or professional community. Many madams and bawds were former prostitutes who had successfully moved up in the hierarchy. Society, of course, did not view their success as praiseworthy; on the contrary, many reformers, American and European alike, believed that one way to end prostitution was to put down "the trade of the brothel keeper," who lived in luxury, "surrounded by beautiful and accomplished young ladies, who for money sell flesh, blood, and soul, that the mistress . . . may not be angered."[20]

Madams and brothel keepers usually contracted with the business community for goods and services on a large scale. This included renting from "respectable" property owners the boarding houses used as brothels or parlor houses. It was generally agreed by all the chroniclers of early California that "it was the holders of real estate that made the greatest fortunes," largely from the high rents charged to brothel keepers. Those who had been able to buy lots in 1848 and early 1849 recovered the full expenditure in one year's rent. Even those who had to rebuild over and over because of fires did not suffer financial loss for any longer than it took to erect a new structure.[21] A study published in 1908 estimated that these real-estate investors made an annual profit of three million dollars in the last decade of the century. The Empire House, a crib that cost $8 thousand to construct, paid out $127,750 a year on the investment; the French Restaurant represented an investment of $400 thousand and still made the owners a high profit. Despite the fact that real-estate investors made their fortunes directly from prostitution, their reputation in society did not suffer. Unlike madams, procurers, and cadets, they were pillars of the business community, often among the most important men in the city—such as the city officials who owned the Municipal crib.

As in many phases of the institution, "respectability" was based on the sex, race, and wealth of the offender.[22] Numerous columns were written about female visitors to assignation houses or women who owned or ran brothels. The "old Houseman keeps the notorious French prostitute in his house, on Clay, opposite Spofford Street, to practice her infamous calling," *Sunday Varieties* reported on September 7, 1856. The woman was "notorious," her calling "infamous," but the man who kept her and the house was merely "old." *Varieties* also reported a crib and grog house run by a German woman, whose husband—according to the paper—understandably shunned her. Similar newspaper articles throughout the period criticized women who ran beer dives, assignation boarding houses, or saloons. Men in the same occupations were apparently not considered newsworthy.[23]

Procurers, on the other hand, were universally despised, no matter what their sex, but it was usually only women or Chinese procurers who made the news. The Mexican "woman of bad character" who tried to "barter the virtue of her daughter" for five hundred dollars in gold was a typical example. In this case, the reporter believed the buyer was the victim: he guessed that the woman was not the girl's mother and that "the girl had no virtue to sell!"[24] However, procurers were considered necessary to the institution: Their role was not only to supply new prostitutes for the brothels but also to handle police payoffs and to secure legal counsel or pay fines when the prostitute was arrested.[25]

The estimates of prices paid to the procurers for women range from twenty-five to two thousand dollars, according to the source, the period, and the condition of the sale. No definite fee is recorded for the ships' captains who brought Latin American women to San Francisco. Prices are equally obscure for Chinese prostitutes procured in the early years. Two Australian women sold on the docks in 1850, however, brought fifteen dollars apiece. Later in the century, Edholm reported professional seducers sold prostitutes for twenty-five to fifty dollars.[26] In the 1890s, when she was writing, the supply of prostitutes in San Francisco was high—it was a buyer's market.

The 1880s and 1890s, on the other hand, were decades of Chinese exclusion, so that to procure Chinese prostitutes was difficult. One account notes that young Chinese girls sold for one hundred to five hundred dollars as domestic slaves; those sold to "houses of ill-fame brought much larger sums." Another writer, referring to the same period, claimed young Chinese prostitutes "on the Pacific Coast have been sold for from $500 to $2,000 each." Of course, Chinese prostitutes were sold into indenture, but the law of supply and demand was still the dominant factor.[27]

Passage of the Mann Act in 1910 and various local and state red-light abatement acts between 1910 and 1914 did little to end prostitution; they merely closed many of the houses. The prostitutes primarily became either call girls, making their appointments by telephone, or streetwalkers, and pimps took over most of the duties the madams and bawds had handled.[28] To keep prostitutes in line, pimps often used physical threats or brutality or would withhold affection from their prostitute. However, by paying her pimp for sexual services and protection, the prostitute gained an important change in roles. Always the seller, she was now the buyer.[29]

As prostitution became more visible during the last decades of the nineteenth century, with designated red-light districts, the numbers of reformers, vice investigators, rescue-mission workers, and religious groups grew with it. In their own way, the efforts of these people were also economic enterprises that flourished because of prostitution. Street preachers, relying on donations from passersby, began in 1849 to demand an end to the wickedness and sin in gold-rush San Francisco.[30] By 1859, the House of Refuge was organized to reform prostitutes. This organization was viewed with justifiable skepticism, since during that period a "fallen woman" was still considered lost forever. The fact that the organization received funds from the city for its work prompted a reporter to question the motives involved "when they [were] well aware that prostitutes, whitewashed by a house of refuge, are fit for no society but that which lies in the graveyard."[31]

By 1869 the ladies of the Methodist Church had organized a mission to aid Chinese prostitutes. Since the Chinese were considered "poor celestial slaves," sympathy and financial support were easier to get. But there might also have been some truth to the conclusion of one writer that "white prostitutes . . . would have met intrusions with a flood of billingsgate worthy of the impudence which prompted such visits—if not a bit of hairpulling or a well-deserved slap in the face."[32] It is interesting to note that when Mary Edholm began her mission work in the 1890s, she made no attempt to rescue or aid experienced prostitutes.

Even so, Edholm did not lightly take up her mission of

reformer among the fallen. She worried that "in this rescue work you must mingle among these degraded ones and I fear for my reputation."[33] Edholm's fears were typical of the new reformers in the 1890s. During the second half of the nineteenth century, charity work among middle-class women was usually confined to such "proper" functions as raising funds to build a church or supporting orphanages. In 1860, ladies' magazines were urging the middle-class woman "not to aid, but to sympathize with the down-trodden. Passive feeling is all that is suitable for elegant females." Consequently when, at the end of the century, women like Edholm, Cameron, and Jane Addams began to work actively and publicly among the "degraded ones," a new outlook on the proper place for women in society was called for.[34]

The fact that women involved in settlement house and rescue-mission work confined their activities to prostitutes who could be defined as victims was understandable; the work was reassuringly respectable. They could probably see for themselves that to approach adult prostitutes with an offer of rescue or rehabilitation was to invite a spirited and "impudent" rebuff.

Although mission and settlement-house workers supported themselves and their activities as a result of the existence of "vice," they were clearly in a different category from the business and professional people who profited from prostitution. Their funds, solicited by lectures, sermons, and printed tracts, were not directly generated by prostitutes. Nevertheless, as with others on the fringe of prostitution, their activities and occupations were dependent on the institution.

What is clear in looking at the many economic sectors of a nineteenth-century city like San Francisco is that prostitution was not a separate economic subculture. Some cities, such as Denver, tried to separate prostitution from the rest of the city by restricting it to a given area, but the institution was not simply a matter of individual prostitutes, their madams, or their cadets. It was a large-scale and widely ramified business based, like all businesses, upon financial gain, and the profits from prostitution were woven intricately throughout society's business and social community. The multiplier effect applies to prostitution as well as to other businesses.

VII. San Francisco Society: The Victorian Influence

In 1851, Albert Benard de Russailh wryly observed that "there are . . . some honest women in San Francisco but not very many."[1] His statement suggests that prostitutes, not "honest women," were more visible in 1851. Having looked at the society of the nineteenth century, the style of living, the economic opportunities, and the changing role of women, we can assume that San Francisco prostitutes might have reflected, as did Hubert H. Bancroft, that "there were some good fellows among the latter-day rich men, but not many."[2] There seemed to be far more "good fellows" among the early-day rich men. The difference, however, lay not in the character of the individual man or woman; rather, it represented social change.

It is difficult to document the attitude of the prostitutes toward their profession, because few left journals, diaries, or memoirs. We can, however, draw some conclusions from what we have been able to learn about the society they lived in.

Although the Victorians did not see themselves as hypocrites—and with the advantage of time and objectivity, we may not see them that way either—to San Francisco's prostitutes, even that city's Victorians must have appeared hypocritical. Critics have pointed out that Victorians professed one way of life and privately practiced another. Prostitutes were part of the private life but often the condemned subjects of the professed life. Politicians were the most culpable; they visited brothels at night and delivered antivice speeches during the day. Commercial sex was even defended by law-enforcement officials on the grounds that it prevented crimes of rape by giving men a sexual outlet outside of marriage.[3] Polite society banished members of the demimonde and yet welcomed their customers. The prostitutes sold a service to those who sought it, but were labeled whores and harlots who lured men into sin.

Respectable women tried to ignore the existence of prostitutes even as they copied their fashions in dress. Law-enforcement officials knew prostitution was illegal, but took bribes and special favors to protect it from the law.

These contradictions occasionally drew public criticism, but not to defend the prostitute's position. The objection was that the male customers escaped blame and retribution. In England, for example, William Acton viewed as absurd the "painful fiction" of punishing only the prostitutes because they were the seducers:

> *The result is practically that the consequences to the male being known and finite, thousands of men suffer themselves to be seduced—as the law has it—by designing women, who sacrifice not only their own future peace of mind and temporal prospects, but court the scorn of the world and bodily suffering to gratify inordinate passion—the unfortunate male is the victim, and by curious perversion the manufacture of prostitutes by female labour is rampant.*[4]

Acton found the law ironic, especially since it was linked with bastardy laws, which held men liable for support of children born out of wedlock. Either men were weak victims of seduction and therefore not responsible even for children or they were equally guilty. Whichever the case, Acton's solution was to fine all men what the traffic would bear. Such punishment, he felt, would either force men to pay heavily for supporting the institution of prostitution or "harden men's hearts against female seductions."[5]

One-sided laws had not always been the case: in seventeenth-century American society, both men and women were punished for committing adultery. By the eighteenth century, however, the situation began to change. In more and more cases, only the woman was punished, while her male companion was acquitted—a development of the attitude that female promiscuity was equivalent to deviance.

This altered view of women was temporarily suspended in the first few years of the gold rush, when any member of the female sex was a welcome sight in San Francisco. As a result, all women were treated with consideration. Since most prostitutes who came to San Francisco had worked in other cities, this reception was a new experience. Men would pay for their company with or *without* sex.[6]

Observers so often described these prostitutes as "flaunting in their gay attire"; "richly dressed, . . . sweeping along, apparently proud of being recognized"; and "flaunting women of pleasure," that it was apparent that their attitude was one of pride and self-confidence.[7] Another observer insisted that "women of the demi-monde who came here in the early days were of the better class: that is they were women who had fallen from a better sphere than did many women of that class, not so much of the rude and vulgar kind."[8]

Were the first San Francisco prostitutes a better class or were they merely treated as a better class? There is no evidence to support the notion that prostitutes of the gold-rush days were less the "rude and vulgar kind." There are indications, however, that they were treated with less rudeness and less vulgarity than prostitutes of the Barbary Coast era later in the century. By the 1860s, women were no longer scarce, and prostitutes were no longer the most visible women present. Some men did "hesitate to walk the street beside a prostitute" once the social restraints of respectable society were imposed.[9] "Women of pleasure" found themselves referred to as "women of their sort." This change in attitude apparently altered the self-image of the prostitute. There were no further descriptions of proud women, sweeping along the street, flaunting their gay attire.

However, one point on which all observers agreed was the comparative lack of social restraints in that city, even after the gold-rush days. As long as one did not interfere with others, there was little condemnation. This situation both fascinated and appalled critics such as the Reverend A. H. Tevis, to whom "No part of our great country [had] a more refined immorality than the Pacific Coast."[10] He found representatives of every ethnic culture "under the sun," as well as prostitutes, gamblers, adventurers, instant millionaires, and those who never lost hope of becoming millionaires. "This adventurous class of men have given a character to the whole Pacific Coast that is worldwide and that will continue through many decades."[11]

Immigrants to California shared a sense of adventure, a willingness to endure the hardships of the frontier for the chance to make a fortune.[12] Having rejected, at least temporarily, settled society, the immigrants seemed reluctant to establish similar social conditions in their exciting new environment. Thus the instability of the social order in San Francisco can be traced to the temperament of the men and women who immigrated there.[13]

Successful eastern businessmen or midwestern farmers with productive lands seldom gave up their secure existence for a chance to search for gold. It would not be inaccurate, then, to say that in San Francisco society there were many former failures, but they were failures who saw opportunities for a second chance. Some succeeded in making their fortune and remained in California, becoming influential in the state's business and political life. Others stuck with their original intention, returning home with the proceeds from their mining. And some continued to try their luck, perpetually confident of eventual success.[14]

Some adventurers cared less about success than they did about being part of the excitement and challenge of the new society. Restless, seeking change and escape from social restraints, they found what they were looking for in the new frontier. All of the factors that led people to immigrate were important to the society that was to develop in the West, and the experiences they shared helped to shape their social views.[15]

Lloyd, usually a severe critic of the frontier character,

recognized that often the new environment changed the people:

> *The change in life effected a change in their beliefs—they found the difference between true worth and "make believe." Their acquaintance with pure ore made them tell at a glance the base-metal—they had no mercy for hypocrisy. They did not pretend to be good; there was in their hearts a lingering idea that the good people were behind them; . . . But their new modes of life developed traits of character which a refined civilization would not have done.*[16]

There were exceptions to the generalization that the immigrants sought a new society, or at least an altered society, in the West. Some wished, and indeed intended, to bring with them that which epitomized refinement and civilized behavior. This group was primarily women, and their desire to cling to what was familiar to them was understandable.

Many of the women who accompanied their husbands or fathers did so because they considered it their duty. Their ability and courage in facing the dangers and hardships of pioneering were magnificent, but their motivation was not adventure and possible riches; rather it was the support of men's need for adventure. They may have anticipated the possibility of wealth and what it would mean when they returned East, but their role in the *quest* for gold was passive. It was the men who dug for gold, an entirely new role for them; women performed the same task of homemaker in a rough environment devoid of the comforts they had left behind. It was hardly surprising that they demanded household conveniences and social refinements as soon as they could be acquired.[17]

Other women shared the sense of adventure. Eliza Farnham was not only capable of accepting a new life but prepared to make the most of the experience. An equally adventurous woman was Louise Clappe. The *Shirley Letters,* which she wrote to her sister in 1854, reveal a pioneer woman whose spirit of adventure helped her to accept every hardship and discomfort with humor and courage. Women like Farnham and Clappe added to the variety of California's and San Francisco's population.

However, what made San Francisco society unusual was not its variety but the fact that it did not separate into leaders and followers until decades after its founding. No clear, consistent segment influenced all others. For every newspaper that was a voice for one set of cultural values, there was an equally influential advocate for another. Even eastern Victorians in San Francisco were unable to maintain the conformity and rational order that were the hallmarks of that culture, since there was no established Victorian society to move into. In the East, the spokesmen for Victorian culture had been the bourgeois elite, who recruited their members from the new industrial rich. In the West, the only rich were the nouveau riche, and though they often tried to emulate the eastern elite, there was no old society to make the rules. The immigrants, of course, had been affected by the predominant culture of their home place; whether European, Asian, eastern Victorian, or southern aristocratic, they brought part of that culture with them to contribute to the "heterogeneous mass" in San Francisco. At various periods throughout the second half of the nineteenth century, rich businessmen controlled the economic life of the city, machine politicians controlled municipal functions, and after 1870 the wives of the railroad barons developed into a social elite—the standard-bearers in fashion, decorum, and cultural pursuits. The leaders in each of these divisions, however, changed constantly throughout the period.[18]

That more than half the people in San Francisco were foreign born unquestionably contributed to the failure of any single group to maintain social leadership. According to the 1860 federal census, 49.91 percent of the population in San Francisco was native born, 50.09 percent foreign born; in California as a whole, 52 percent was native born, 48 percent foreign born. No other state in the nation had such a high percentage of foreign-born residents. Wisconsin and Minnesota were the next highest with 35 percent and 33 percent, respectively, but because most of those immigrants were from Scandinavian countries, the national culture and characteristics of those countries exerted a predominant influence. In California, and especially in San Francisco, however, no one immigrant group was large enough to rule, yet few were so small that they were forced to assimilate into a larger American culture. Chinese, Latin Americans, French, Germans, and Irish were only a few of the cultures present in numbers large enough to form visible segments of the society of San Francisco.[19]

Among the native-born population, the largest group, 30 percent, came from the Northeast; the Midwest supplied 20 percent; the South, 15 percent. (The remaining 35 percent were native Californians.)[20] Although the Northeast had the widest representation and exerted some influence, primarily Victorian cultural values, over social views in San Francisco, the yankees were unable to overshadow the other segments of the society. The spirit of independence that marked the population produced leaders, not followers. San Franciscans were speculators not content to work for someone else; otherwise, they would not have been part of the California migration. Wage labor was not their habit "and the individuals who [did] it never regard[ed] it as a settled business, but [were] always . . . looking about for some better chance."[21]

This sense of adventure, independence, and individualism was reinforced in the early days by the pace of living. Each individual had to find his share of the gold before someone else did. A city had to be built so that one could fully enjoy the riches coming out of the Sierra. But that city had to supply only opportunities for business and pleasure, not residential neighborhoods—most individuals did not come to San Francisco for community and were not initially susceptible to community influences: "The people, as a community, had run riot in everything. There was no apparent unity among them. But individually, each was at work, desperately in earnest; and out of this chaotic life, though not yet perceptible, were springing order and true prosperity."[22]

Lloyd continually referred to the spirited, restless character of the early San Franciscans, examining the society he was part of, searching for explanations. His writings demonstrate that he was more attuned to Victorian conformity and rational order than he was to the chaotic excitement of San Francisco. His search for a rational explanation for the society he observed is in itself revealing. One passage describes the dominant, persistent values, the antithesis of Victorianism: "Every one was free to do whatsoever he chose, if he did not interfere with anybody else, and his conduct was not questioned. So it was that in the absence of a restraining sentiment they gave full sway to their passions and desires."[23]

Lloyd was condemning, not praising, San Franciscans for this trait. The authors of the *Annals,* more a part of the gold-rush society, made similar observations—with one important difference: they applauded the very forty-niner characteristics that Lloyd criticized:

> *There was no sauntering, no idleness, no dreaming. All was practical and real; all energy, perseverance and success. In business and in pleasure, the San Franciscans were* fast *folk; . . . A month with them was considered equal to a year with other people. In the former short time [1849–1851] men did such deeds, and saw, felt, thought, suffered and enjoyed, as much as would have lasted over a twelvemonth in other lands. But then these were really men.*[24]

Nor was the admiration expressed in the *Annals* reserved for the men. "Like the male inhabitants," the journal noted, "the females of San Francisco are among the finest specimens, physically, of the sex, that can anywhere be seen."[25]

San Franciscans were proud of their accomplishments, of their independence, and of the freedom from "the salutary checks of a high moral public opinion" found in the East.[26] Some were even proud of their "wicked reputation," not from a preference for vice but because they viewed it as a symbol of their lack of hypocrisy:

> *Though there be much vice in San Francisco, one virtue—though perhaps a negative one, the citizens at least have. They are not hypocrites, who pretend to high qualities which they do not possess. In great cities of the old world, or it may be even in those of the pseudo-righteous New England States, there may be quite as much crime and vice committed as in San Francisco, only the customs of the former places throw a decent shade over the grosser, viler aspects. The criminal, the fool, and the voluptuary are not allowed to boast, directly or indirectly, of their bad, base, or foolish deeds, as is so often done in California. . . . Many things that are considered morally and socially wrong by others at*

a distance, are not so viewed by San Franciscans when done among themselves. It is the hurt done to a man's own conscience that often constitutes the chief harm of an improper action; and if San Franciscans conscientiously think that, after all, their wild and pleasant life is not so very, very wrong, neither is it so really and truly wrong.[27]

As long as the spirit of the forty-niner—the independent individualist—remained part of the San Francisco character, there was little development of community consciousness. The vigilance committees and the fire brigades were able to organize for short periods and specific goals, but the need for each stemmed directly from a lack of municipal police and fire protection. Typical San Franciscans believed that everyone had the right "to do whatsoever he chose, if he did not interfere with anyone else," a belief hardly conducive to the development of community spirit. This attitude, occasionally viewed by visitors as callous, was interpreted as a mark of respect among adults. There is a certain sense of paternalism and condescension manifest when individuals or groups adopt the attitude of being their brother's keeper. In a society composed primarily of adult males in the prime of life, the assumption was (until proven otherwise) that their brothers did not need a keeper.[28] When it was clear that someone needed help, such help was always given freely. Letters, diaries, and journals of the period frequently note the easy generosity of the pioneers.

Some San Franciscans were so unconventional that they mourned the famed courtesan, Julia Bulette, when she was murdered in Virginia City, Nevada.[29] Others were so righteous that they criticized the play *Camille* because it was the story of the "clap-trap sufferings" of a fallen woman.[30] What appear to be inconsistencies in San Franciscans were merely independent viewpoints being given equal coverage; they were in no way expected to reflect a consensus.

Superficial values such as etiquette or appearance lost significance in the course of the journey West. Eliza Farnham, who was in many ways part of the Victorian culture, reminded women that clothes had very little to do with being a lady. She pointed out that every overland pioneer woman could relate hardships that would make her eastern sisters faint in horror. But despite months on the trail performing "all the coarser offices that properly belong to the other sex"—yoking oxen, foraging for food, dressing in tattered clothing—women remained soft-spoken, gentle, and feminine if they were true ladies.[31]

Another spokeswoman for Victorianism in San Francisco, Mrs. Day of the *Hesperian,* did not waste time reminding people to eat with a fork rather than a knife, as some eastern etiquette books recommended. Her prescriptions for an improved quality of life were much more basic: schools and churches had to be built, homes and family ties needed strengthening, and it was left to the pioneer women to accomplish these goals.[32]

The harshest criticism the San Francisco Victorians leveled against women was directed toward those who did not join their husbands in the West when urged to do so. They were warned that they had only themselves to blame when their husbands became "openly debauched" or considered "themselves alone again, the family ties permanently broken, the marital and paternal obligations dissolved and themselves free." In proper Victorian manner, such women were reminded that it was their duty to come "to the country which is the home of those you are bound to adhere to and save." The overly genteel lady, however, would find herself sadly out of place should she be unable to cultivate the courage to face the "pains and perils" of the move.[33]

As the century progressed and transportation improved, such admonitions were no longer necessary. By the time the transcontinental railroad was completed, the motives for moving West had changed. Most who came West after the Civil War were settlers, and the influence of Victorianism began to increase. As a result, the prescriptive literature which had enjoyed such a long hegemony in the East began to exert more influence in the West. Advising women on their duties in the home was especially important, because San Francisco remained primarily a hotel and boarding-house community. Benjamin Lloyd reasoned that the slow growth of private homes was because men of domestic habits were rare, "and women have come to regard family cares and duties as a sort of drudgery without [outside] their province."[34]

Traditional home life in San Francisco was also undermined by the number of divorces.[35] Some critics blamed women who did not have housekeeping duties to keep them busy. It was believed that they grew restless and, succumbing to the town's loose morals, "kept company" with other men. The more outspoken advocates of Victorian values believed the prevalence of divorce in San Francisco was a direct result of the community's failure to censure and ostracize "unprincipled husbands and wives." Another explanation for the higher divorce rate in California was women's constitutional right to own property. With property of their own, women were no longer dependent on their husbands for survival. With such important problems to deal with, advocates of Victorianism in the West could hardly be expected to spend much time with such trivial matters as fashion and demure conduct.

It was on the subject of divorce that Lloyd became the most outraged—and outrageous. In organizing his book, he included the subjects of divorce and sudden death in the same chapter. Such an arrangement was not for any definite purpose, he claimed, but

> *if by any suggestiveness the combination contains, any one should be deterred from committing so grave a social crime as divorce, it will have proven a happy accident. It is not always that sudden death follows so closely upon divorce, but if by chance or otherwise it should occur so frequently as to be looked upon as ominous and become a superstition, it would certainly do much to check the tide of family disruption.*[36]

With such subjects as morals, divorce, and the family, Lloyd was comfortably at home with Victorian values. He did, however, display a grudging respect for the independent traits that kept some San Franciscans from being hypocrites and for the industry they showed in recovering from the city's recurrent, devastating fires.

Visitors to the West found it easier to maintain a more consistently Victorian viewpoint. Sallie Snow, during her

1868 visit to San Francisco, wrote to her sister making it clear that she preferred to keep to herself rather than associate with a society that did not meet her standards of proper ethnic origin and social refinement, often synonymous criteria to the typical Victorian: "I am very unfavorably situated as regards society there being none that I care to cultivate in the immediate vicinity. As Irish or Germen [sic] though of good class but Catholic or Jews. Very respectable quiet neighborhood but—of course I cannot be intimate with any of them."[37]

Isabelle Saxon, a British visitor, was subtly prescriptive, couching her criticisms and advice in statements of praise. Because of their sudden wealth and a lack of home duties (because of hotel living), women in California, Saxon observed, had a sad tendency toward overdressing and ostentation: "Americans are notoriously a very generous people, and it is saddening to see their love of display darkening the pristine simplicity of a noble republicanism, and that to the extent it assuredly does at the present day."[38] Although admiring pristine simplicity, Saxon also praised the "luxuries of all kinds" available in San Francisco to those of wealth. Unfortunately, she returned to England before seeing the "palaces of the rich" in New York[39] or the California railroad magnates' Nob Hill mansions.

If she thought the love of display in 1861 was saddening, what might she have said about homes with walls of a "medieval castle, complete with battlements and towers" or bedrooms "furnished in ebony and inlaid with ivory and 'semi-precious stones' "?[40] Jane Lathrop Stanford, Mary Sherwood Hopkins, and Arabella Yarrington Huntington, wives of three railroad kings, established a social order similar to that of the eastern cities. The homes they built on Nob Hill were more lavish, more opulent than others around them. These women, in emulating eastern social standards, sought to be as influential in the social world as were their husbands in the railroad empire. (Arabella Huntington was already part of the eastern elite when she married.) With improved transportation, the elite of San Francisco society could travel comfortably to refined cultural centers such as New York, Boston, and London, where they eventually acquired many superficial Victorian values that had earlier escaped the West.[41]

By the 1870s, however, the values associated with Victorianism had begun to change, as contradictory forces altered society and forced changes upon these values. By the 1870s, proper women were no longer restricted to the home. Although their primary roles were still wife, mother, moral guide, and custodian of the "good" virtues, before they married, they could work outside the home without losing "caste." Young women of middle-class families began working in offices as clerks and "lady typewriters" or as teachers or social workers. As these daughters of the middle class began moving into occupations outside the home, it became necessary for their families to alter their view of the proper role for women. They could no longer assume that working women were either destitute or less than respectable. Furthermore, women like Mary Anderson, a shoe worker who became director of the U.S. Woman's Bureau, Jane Addams of Hull House, Mary Edholm and Donaldina Cameron of San Francisco, no longer narrowly confined to the home, experiencing new social situations and ideas, began to add their voices to earlier protests against the confining social standards and work opportunities for women.[42]

At various times, women had openly opposed the laws and customs that mandated one set of restrictions for them and another for men. Abigail Adams, in a letter to her husband, requested the writers of the Constitution not to give husbands unlimited power over their wives. In 1848, Elizabeth Cady Stanton, Susan B. Anthony, and others demanded suffrage and property rights. And the double standard of morality was roundly criticized, especially in the last quarter of the century, by suffrage and women's-rights supporters as well as by male and female settlement workers. Before Victorian culture (with its advocacy of public conformity) predominated, agitation against the double standard was more frequent. In the 1830s the New York Female Moral Reform Society worked actively to close down houses of prostitution and in this way confront the larger issue of "the double standard, and the male sexual license it condoned."[43]

The Victorians, however, had developed a different set of values. Culture was public and prescriptive; therefore, one did not blatantly agitate against its inconsistencies. Instead, proper behavior was stressed through works of fiction and advice articles, with only occasional messages against the double standard. (This is not to suggest that the inconsistencies in moral standards were ignored during the Victorian era, but there was less open discussion and protest in the ladies' journals and magazines than before 1850 or after 1875.) In the West, however, opposition was far more consistent throughout the whole second half of the century.[44]

The topic of the double standard was a continuing subject in San Francisco. There were, for example, a series of letters to the editor of the *Bulletin* deploring the morals of young men who behaved with propriety to their ladies and then spent the night "at some house up town of character." The editor condemned the "double style" for men, wives, and "harlots" and endorsed the view that men should not escape ostracism by society: "Ladies of refinement . . . exclude, with commendable contempt and disgust, the frail woman"; they should, he declared, treat the libertine in the same manner.[45]

During the years that she published and edited the *Hesperian*, Day continually opposed the double standard. Her stance, however, was more militant than that of the *Bulletin*. An advertisement in the local newspapers (in 1858) invited ladies to take part in a horseback-riding contest. They were assured of being free from "improper associations," because no woman would be allowed to enter without a card issued by the committee. Day urged women to boycott the event.

> *Can it be that it [the card] is to secure woman from association with the unfortunate of her own sex? If so, what protection is offered her against the base and degraded of the other sex? We confess, in our humble judgement, we can see no great difference in an association with an unfortunate and degraded sister, and an association with the vile, miserable, heartless villain who made her what she is.*[46]

A few months later, Day took up the subject in a series of articles on social evils:

> *The evils we suffer under, we alone can remedy—the cure is in our own hands. We refuse to associate with a fallen and degraded woman; the ban of society has gone forth against her; and, though she repent in dust and ashes, and bathe herself in the bitter tears of re-*

> *pentance, still is heard the cry, 'unclean!' . . . But how is* he *treated who brought about this sorrow? . . . Instead of being spurned from society with his unhappy victims, his presence is too often courted, and he is received with smiles and caresses. . . . Retaliate for the wrong done our sex as though we were but* one woman.[47]

For Day to give her opinions without a conciliating introduction was unusual and suggests an emotionalism she was usually careful not to manifest. Although she did not openly advocate welcoming the "degraded woman" back into society, the implication was there in her own editorials as well as the articles of others that she printed. Nor did she place full responsibility for upholding public morality on women. If women were supposed to be weak and need the protection of men, then men had to take their share of responsibility for protecting the purity and innocence they professed to admire. "You guard her carefully from the society of the impure of her own sex, yet place her directly within the influence and in the power of heartless, degraded men. Repine not if your inconsistency is visited upon your own head."[48]

Later in the century, Harriet Stevens, in a prize-winning essay, took a more traditional approach, predicting that change would occur as a result of man's association with women in the business world. "Women are now [1892] found everywhere—behind the counter, in the counting room, in the telegraph office, and other places of business, as well as in the home, the law office, the physician's closet and the studio of the artist, and everywhere their influence has been to refine the men with whom they associate."[49] Although Stevens did not condemn or demand an end to the double standard, her essay clearly foresaw a time of equality in moral obligations when men made greater contact with "the moral world which is woman's."

Despite the protests and predictive messages, the double standard was perpetuated by Victorian society's pretense that no respectable men visited nonrespectable women. Lloyd, for example, commented that the ladies would be indignant if they knew their wealthy and respected husbands visited houses of ill fame, but the "consternation among the belles of society would be assumed for effect."[50] They knew their men spent time with fallen women, and yet they "smiled upon them [the men] and gave them countenance." Lloyd expected women to put an end to such immorality by condemning the "fallen brother" as they did the "fallen sister."

However, repentance and salvation or rehabilitation were not thought possible until later in the century. The rescue-mission worker Mary Edholm urged forgiveness and the acceptance of the fallen back into society. To make her point, she recorded what she claimed was the speech of a man to the woman he was going to marry.

> *Well darling, you are not half so bad as I, because you fell under promise of marriage, and would gladly have been a wife, if that scoundrel had not deserted you—but I! I have wronged a girl and then basely deserted her. I have been the base deceiver, and somewhere in the world—maybe in a haunt of shame—I have a child who would have starved for anything I have done for it. You have been noble enough to care for your child, while I have neglected my own flesh and blood even when making a large salary. . . . I've been coward enough to let her bear the disgrace and infamy and struggle as a woman must struggle with her pittance of wages to support my child. And you are a thousand times more noble than I. Nor is that all; you were betrayed by a lover who swore most solemnly that he would marry you, and you have never sinned with any other. But I, not content with betraying an innocent girl to infamy, I have frequented houses of shame, just because I wanted to—not because I was deceived or snared into sin as you have been, but just because I did not have manliness enough to conquer my own vicious desires. But unworthy as I am, if you will take me for your husband I will lead a good life and be true to you. You are certainly not half as bad as I am.*[51]

Whether any man actually made such a statement is open to question. The change of attitude Edholm's report conveyed, however, is revealing. The double standard should be abolished not because immoral men were as bad as immoral women (as earlier protests stressed), but because both could reform. Additionally, there was the reminder that no

Christian has the right to condemn. The suggestion that a *manly* man would not frequent "houses of shame" was also different from the idea that a "good" man would not do so. Men had always been forgiven any lapse in moral behavior on the premise that men were naturally base and that only a good woman could save them from themselves. Edholm clearly supported this theory, only in her example the "good" woman had at one time been a fallen woman.

Neither Day, Lloyd, Edholm, nor any of the other writers who pointed out the inequities of the double standard succeeded in banishing it from society. In fact, separate moral judgements for men and women were more rigid than that prevailing in San Francisco of the 1850s. The spirit of the pioneer, however, was not completely subordinated; the "heterogeneous mass" was merely quelled slightly by the voice of conformity and rational order.

VIII. EPILOGUE

Historians until recently have ignored prostitution as a topic of interest. Most studies have been conducted by sociologists and psychologists. Sociologists usually sought broad-based trends: how many prostitutes were there in cities of comparable size? did they share similar backgrounds? and so on. Psychologists' questions often focused on the motivation of individual prostitutes, and their explanations for "why women become prostitutes" range from masochism to Freudian complexes. Prostitutes, however, continue to give the same answer to the question that their counterparts gave in earlier times: women prostitute themselves to make money.[1]

Financial gain is the one explanation that has been a constant throughout the history of prostitution. While sociological and psychological studies haven't ignored this response by prostitutes, they have used the economic as a stepping stone for social commentary. Among other things, they evoke urban economics and social deviancy, both of which are valid explanations, but neither contributes much to an understanding of the prostitutes' point of view. Prostitutes today claim that they are able to enjoy some luxuries as well as pay for their college education by acting as call girls or working in massage parlors.[2] Beverly Davis, a twentieth-century madam, dealing with more than her own motives claimed, "As for the type of girls who work as prostitutes—probably then as now—they go into the life because they want to. They want to earn a lot of money. I found, as a madam contracting thousands, they wouldn't be stenographers and saleswomen if they could."[3] And James Garniss reported in the 1850s that the only regret one prostitute in San Francisco had after making $50,000 was "that she had not double capacity for increasing her gains."[4]

Twentieth-century prostitutes have been very outspoken in their defiance of the psychological experts and their explanations. In commenting on the view that prostitutes, especially those with pimps, are merely punishing themselves, Sally Stanford, one of the last madams of San Francisco, offered the argument that appears generally to be accepted by prostitutes. "I might accept this point of view if I could work up some substantial respect for the psychiatrists themselves, many of whom make headlines for . . . charging their frustrated female patients for their sexual services on the couch."[5] Stanford's main objection was that no one questioned the assumption from which the psychological explanations proceed.

Prostitution, according to such views, is behavior deviant from the social norms, or in this case, the moral standards. The idea of moral deviancy is accepted before the motives of the women are examined. But history is quite clear on the point that morality is not a constant. It is, as Stanford defined it, "just a word that describes the current fashion of conduct." It does not even describe the conduct of *all* people at any given period. The Victorians had a very rigid set of moral standards, but it would be absurd to imagine that everyone living between 1850 and 1900 subscribed to their notions. Is it then correct to condemn as deviant the prostitute who voluntarily enters the profession and does not "worry about being immoral in someone's daffy code book"?[6]

Prostitution in San Francisco in the days of the gold rush differed from the same trade as practiced in the established urban areas of the country in that San Francisco had no standards of conduct to deviate from. As the town became a metropolis, changes occurred; families demanded modes of conduct that were familiar to them, and proper conduct relegated prostitution to improper behavior. San Francisco had to change, but it did so gradually and never with the unanimous support of the population.

No matter which period of San Francisco history one studies, one point recurs regularly. Changes in attitudes toward prostitutes were brought about by individuals or small groups of individuals rather than by any large segment of the population. Because Irene McCready drew attention to herself, a handful of ladies were forced to state their objections to public women at private functions. The Bella Cora incident inspired complaints about notorious women at public places only because a United States Marshal was shot. And the closing of bordellos in the Barbary Coast and enforcement of the Red-light Abatement Act resulted from the indignation that Reverend Paul Smith aroused after he had been solicited by a prostitute in that area.[7]

When the public had a chance to express its views, such as in the election of mayors, it did not vote down vice. Instead, the people elected men like Jimmy Rolph (mayor in 1911), who promised a wide-open town. Rolph's response to prostitution was to "leave it alone; just regulate it." According to Sally Stanford, San Franciscans were pleased with things as they were, and the changes that finally came were not brought about by them. World War II brought an influx of people from "Paducah, Peoria, and Pocatello" who were fascinated by the city. But they "brought their Midwest or down East small-town standards too, the jerks. As soon as they had established enough residence to enable them to vote, they voted like the provincials they were, for purity, and started the destruction of the spirit of the colorful city that had fascinated them."[8]

What Stanford saw as the destruction of the San Francisco spirit merely led to another change in the institution of prostitution. By skimming the daily paper, one can ascertain that the profession is still flourishing and still reflecting society's attitude toward sexuality and toward women. And prostitution in San Francisco is still just slightly different from that in other places.

San Francisco was the birthplace of one of the first prostitutes' unions in the United States. COYOTE (an acronym for call off your old tired ethics) in the 1970s was a strong voice for the modern "fair but frail" in the "colorful city." Its founder, retired prostitute Margo St. James, called the first prostitutes' convention in July 1974 in San Francisco. Union membership at the time was reported to be 3,500. The union revived the prostitutes' ball that was part of the city's demimonde tradition one hundred and twenty years before. COYOTE was only one unusual manifestation of the San Francisco spirit. Another was Sally Stanford. Along with many of her predecessors, from Irene McCready to Tessie Wall, Sally was one "all time all timer in the Hall of Ill-fame," as San Francisco columnist Herb Caen wrote. Madam Sally became Madam Mayor of Sausalito, a San Francisco suburb.[9]

Nor did the brothel tradition completely disappear in the "city that knows how." In 1975, a Victorian house on Bush Street, furnished in crimson silk, damask, and velvet plush, was raided as a house of ill fame. Keeping abreast of the times, however, it was listed as a sex clinic where weary and harried businessmen could work out their sexual problems with women who were professionals. The clinic was called the Golden Gate Foundation and was licensed by the city to operate an "emotional therapy research foundation." The women who worked for the foundation offered "therapeutic and sex counseling services" and carried gold business cards which promised the "preservation of fine traditions." After long and *thorough* investigation, the San Francisco vice squad concluded that the "red carpeted salon," where customers paid fifty to three hundred dollars for services, was a traditional bordello; they raided the premises and arrested the employees. Another tradition upheld by the police was their failure to arrest the customers.[10]

Between February and August 1983, after twenty months of investigation, San Francisco vice officers arrested fifteen women for prostitution and four entrepreneurs of an escort service that they charged was the "biggest call-girl operation in the state." The newspapers referred to the alleged prostitution empire as a sophisticated multimillion-dollar business employing over a hundred and fifty women. Each woman carried a credit card imprinter with her on the job and, presumably for the sake of even greater efficiency, the company was in the process of becoming computerized at the time of the arrests. The "mastermind of the enterprise" was reported by the *San Francisco Chronicle* to be a former Tenderloin-area prostitute, who was now president of the escort corporation making "profits of millions of dollars."[11] Her reaction to the arrest was to state that she was guilty of nothing more than "success in a field dominated by men." She based her success as a businesswoman on having "used 13 years of hard work and ingenuity to achieve success." Again, there was no report of customers being arrested.

The history of prostitution also reveals changes in public acceptance of the institution. (A poll taken in 1974, for example, showed that 50 percent of the citizens in San Francisco did not "think the prostitution laws should be enforced.")[12] But whether the period is sexually liberal or repressive, segments of society attempt to establish the morality or immorality of sexual practices through legislation.

Legislators in France in the thirteenth century were as determined as those in San Francisco in the nineteenth century and in California in the twentieth century to govern moral conduct and "illicit" sex. And prostitutes and their customers are as determined to circumvent the regulations. The *Annals* commented upon the futility of such efforts in the 1850s: "The common council passed a stringent ordinance regarding houses of ill-fame, making the keeping of them highly penal . . . and then it was found to be utterly unpracticable in operation. It seemed all at once to be discovered, that the impurity which was hid by walls, could not be put down by mere legislation."[13]

Nevertheless, legislators keep trying, passing laws that try once more to control the institution of prostitution. The American Civil Liberties Union has worked through the courts to challenge the constitutionality of prostitution laws. Since 1974, in California and elsewhere, legislative action has removed the penalties against consenting adults who participate in sexual acts that were previously considered immoral and indecent.[14] Such legislative action reflects a change in social attitudes toward sex. It also reflects the more liberal views of the 1970s. Predicting the permanency of such changes and their impact on prostitution is problematic. But, if history is any kind of guide, it is safe to say that attitudes toward prostitution and the role of prostitutes in American society will reflect those changes.

NOTES

PREFACE

1. The definition and usage for *prostitute* and the definitions for terms below that also mean prostitute are taken from James Murray's *A New English Dictionary* (1888) and the *Unabridged Oxford English Dictionary.* Both sources give the etymology and usage of the words at different periods.

2. The term *brothel keeper* was used more commonly by the nineteenth century. Both men and women were brothel keepers.

CHAPTER ONE. INTRODUCTION: A WOMAN'S PLACE

1. Ilse Seibert, *Women in the Ancient Near East,* pp. 38–39.
2. Sarah Pomeroy, *Goddesses, Whores, Wives, and Slaves,* pp. 88, 117.
3. Sir James Frazer, *The New Golden Bough,* pp. 298–300.
4. Amaury de Riencourt, *Sex and Power in History,* p. 132.
5. William W. Sanger, M.D., *The History of Prostitution, Its Extent, Causes, and Effects Throughout the World,* pp. 36–37.
6. Ibid., p. 94.
7. Dr. Fernando Henriques, *Prostitution in Europe and the Americas,* pp. 42, 59; Sanger, *History of Prostitution,* p. 95.
8. Henriques, *Prostitution in Europe and the Americas,* pp. 135–36.
9. Riencourt, *Sex and Power,* pp. 147–51.
10. Ibid., pp. 241–42.
11. Henriques, *Prostitution in Europe and the Americas,* pp. 130–31.
12. Ibid., p. 136.
13. Howard B. Woolston, *Prostitution in the United States,* p. 15.
14. Ibid., pp. 8–9.
15. Clifford Geertz, ed., *Interpretation of Cultures,* p. 5.
16. Daniel Howe, "American Victorianism as a Culture," *American Quarterly* XXVII (December 1975), pp. 521–32.
17. Ibid., pp. 507–09.
18. Ibid., p. 517; Steven Marcus, *The Other Victorians: A Study*

of Sexuality and Pornography in Mid-Nineteenth Century England, and others stress this trait as well.

19. Dee Garrison, "Immoral Fiction," pp. 71, 74.

20. Clifton Furness, *The Genteel Female,* pp. 132–51.

21. Emily Thornwell, *Complete Guide to Gentility;* Furness, *Genteel Female,* pp. 132–51.

22. Marcus, *Other Victorians,* p. 31; Carl N. Degler, "Women's Sexuality in the Nineteenth Century," pp. 1467–68. Both Marcus and Degler are quoting from Acton's work (widely read in the United States), *The Functions and Disorders of the Reproduction Organs in Youth, in Adult Age, and in Advanced Life: Considered in their Physiological, Social, and Psychological Relations.*

23. Degler, "Women's Sexuality," pp. 1467, 1469.

24. Ibid., pp. 1469–70. There were 60 thousand copies of Napheys' book, *The Physical Life of Women: Advice to the Maiden, Wife, and Mother* (1869), in print within the first two years.

25. Degler, "Women's Sexuality," pp. 1483–89. The survey that Degler calls the Mosher survey was admittedly limited; forty-five women were polled over a twenty or twenty-five year period; their geographic origins were based on which schools or colleges they attended; and their exact ages are unknown. Despite these limitations, it is the only survey that questions women of the Victorian period and the Victorian culture on the subject of sexuality; consequently, it is an important addition to the understanding of sexuality among the Victorians. See also *American Heritage* 32 (1981):4.

26. Degler, "Women's Sexuality," pp. 1483–89.

27. Ibid., p. 1477.

28. Marcus, *Other Victorians,* p. 31.

29. Ibid., p. 29.

30. Ibid., pp. 29–31.

31. Acton, *Prostitution,* p. 118.

32. Ibid., p. 160.

33. Marcus, *Other Victorians,* pp. 100–01.

CHAPTER TWO. "THE TIME WAS THE BEST EVER MADE"

1. Eliza Farnham, *California In-Doors and Out,* p. 257.

2. Frank Soulé, John Gihon, M.D., and James Nisbet, *The Annals of San Francisco,* pp. 243–44.

3. Ibid., p. 206.

4. Charles Howe, *Reminiscences,* Bancroft Dictations, Berkeley, California.

5. Soulé, Gihon, and Nisbet, *Annals,* p. 225. Although organized

city services such as fire protection were just getting started in other parts of the country, volunteer brigades had a long history. The need for such services in San Francisco was desperate. Water was scarce, and the entire town was built (five times) out of highly combustible materials.

6. Most primary sources on early San Francisco mention the high cost of living. The examples I have used above are from James Garniss, "The Early Days of San Francisco, 1877," Bancroft Dictations, pp. 15–18; Hubert Howe Bancroft, *Works,* vol. 23, pp. 190–91; Albert Benard de Russailh, *Last Adventure,* p. 10.

7. Bancroft, *Works,* vol. 22, p. 189; Soulé, Gihon, and Nisbet, *Annals,* p. 214.

8. Soulé, Gihon, and Nisbet, *Annals,* p. 216.

9. Garniss, Bancroft Collections, p. 14.

10. Farnham, *California In-Doors and Out,* p. 258.

11. Soulé, Gihon, and Nisbet, *Annals,* p. 666.

12. Bancroft, *Works,* vol. 1, p. 578.

13. Aileen Kraditor, ed., *Up From the Pedestal,* pp. 189–204; Barbara Welter, "The Cult of True Womanhood," in Jean Friedman and William Slade, *Our American Sisters,* pp. 99–123. Both Kraditor and Welter demonstrate how women were constantly instructed in their role as moral protectors of society through ladies' magazines, religious tracts, antisuffrage speeches, and newspaper editorials.

14. Soulé, Gihon, and Nisbet, *Annals,* pp. 259, 656. See also: Garniss, Bancroft Dictations, who recalled how men took off their hats and bowed to the "lewd women of the town" (p. 17); Benjamin E. Lloyd, *Lights and Shades in San Francisco,* p. 147; Elisha O. Crosby, "Events in California," Bancroft Dictations, p. 123, was struck by the unusual "respect and gallantry" extended to prostitutes.

15. Soulé, Gihon, and Nisbet, *Annals,* p. 248.

16. Ibid., p. 250.

17. Ibid., pp. 134, 428.

18. Benard de Russailh, *Last Adventure,* pp. 12–14; Etienne Derbec, *A French Journalist in the California Gold Rush,* p. 167; Farnham, *California In-Doors and Out,* pp. 272–74; Garniss, Bancroft Dictations, pp. 15–16; Soulé, Gihon, and Nisbet, *Annals,* p. 448; Lloyd, *Lights and Shades,* pp. 182–83.

19. Lloyd, *Lights and Shades,* pp. 182–83.

20. *Municipal Reports to the Board of Supervisors 1863–64.* A report by Chief of Police Burke, outlined the attempts by the state to "do something" about gambling. Before March 1851, gambling was public; in March 1852, An Act to License Gambling was passed; in April 1855 it was replaced by An Act to Prohibit Gaming, making

the offense a misdemeanor until 1857, when it became a felony. By 1860, the felony status was removed, and gaming again became a misdemeanor with a minimal fine. In 1863, the legislature seemed to give up the struggle and passed An Act to Confer Further Power Upon the Board of Supervisors, authorizing them to "*prohibit and suppress, or exclude from certain limits all houses of ill-fame, prostitution and gaming.*" The Act allowed San Francisco to control its own "vice" problems. The various ordinances passed by the board of supervisors, reflects (1) times when reformers were in office, (2) times when xenophobia against the Chinese and Mexican was popular, and (3) times when the police were lax in enforcing the laws.

21. Garniss, Bancroft Dictations, pp. 15–16. The average bet in a gambling hall was between fifty cents and five dollars, but Soulé, Gihon, and Nisbet, *Annals* (p. 248) reported that bets from $1 thousand to $116 thousand were not unheard of, and Benard de Russailh, *Last Adventures* (p. 14) claimed he heard of bets up to $20 thousand, though he never saw amounts of gold more than two-hundred ounces ($3,200) being wagered. It was the calm acceptance of winning or losing that surprised the various writers as much as the amounts that were bet. Complacency was not universal, because many of the suicides at the time were believed to be those who had lost large sums gambling (Lloyd, *Lights and Shades*, p. 350). The fact that the casual acceptance of high gambling losses impressed so many observers is, I believe, because loss in one area of speculation was not synonymous with failure. Fortunes were there to be made, if not in one area then in another, and if one opportunity were lost there would be more.

22. Lloyd, *Lights and Shades*, p. 83.

23. Derbec, *French Journalist*, p. 167. The competition among the women was usually between the American and French prostitutes. For a number of reasons, which will be discussed later, French courtesans were the most coveted in San Francisco.

24. Soulé, Gihon, and Nisbet, *Annals*, p. 641. Bancroft, vol. 25, p. 241, claimed the average gambling-hall salary to be $250 per month.

CHAPTER THREE. "THE FAIRER SEX": AMERICAN STYLE

1. Soulé, Gihon, and Nisbet, *Annals*, pp. 668–69.

2. Crosby, Bancroft Collections; Soulé, Gihon, and Nisbet, *Annals;* Lloyd, *Lights and Shades;* and Bancroft, *Works*, remark on the decorous conduct of the prostitutes and the respectability of their customers. But these writers are men who claim never to have been customers in the "gilded palaces" (parlor houses) and who seem to

feel it necessary to seem slightly shocked by the vice hiding itself in "staid dignity." Their suggestion was that the "poor fallen creature" in this setting was grateful to be able to "act and appear as a lady" once more. Had they suggested that the prostitute was pleased to be *treated* as a lady, it would not be difficult to accept this analysis. Given the situation in frontier San Francisco, however, the suggestion that the parlor-house prostitute was envious of other women around her is questionable. She was treated with respect, she was making more money and living in more comfortable surroundings than any other woman in the city. She was also a businesswoman, and she acted and appeared in whatever manner would bring her the most business. The attitude of the writers mentioned above was typical of the nineteenth-century view of prostitutes; it was seldom if ever suggested that any woman voluntarily entered the profession. Even in frontier literature, where prostitutes were generally given more liberal treatment, writers were careful to qualify their complimentary statements by reminding the reader that such women were fallen, lewd, and outcasts of society. The contradiction between description and analysis makes it difficult to present an accurate picture.

3. The Barbary Coast developed after 1865.

4. Soulé, Gihon, and Nisbet, *Annals*, p. 668.

5. These conclusions are drawn from a variety of references throughout the nineteenth century. In addition to sources already cited, see accounts in the daily newspapers of the time: *California Courier*, July 6, 1850; *San Francisco Evening News and Picayune*, November 1, 1853; *Evening Bulletin*, November 18, 1855; *Sunday Varieties*, January 23, 1859; *California Police Gazette*, November 18, 1865, and many others. These sources and various police reports refer to police bribes, the existence of "houses" in residential neighborhoods, and the shrewdness of individual madams.

6. Crosby, Bancroft Collections, pp. 121–23. Gentry's very entertaining journalistic history, *Madams of San Francisco*, discounts the existence of the Countess. Gentry's skepticism is based primarily on his belief that she did not "appear in *any* account until the 1930s." She did in fact appear in Crosby's dictation to Bancroft, (Collections), in which he reminisced about events in California in 1849. One of Gentry's arguments against her existence is based on the fact that the El Dorado, the most lavish establishment in San Francisco, was still housed in a tent in December of 1849, and it is therefore unlikely, he insists, that the Countess presided in better surroundings. Crosby, however, does not claim her house was lavish, merely that it was "a large frame house two stories high." Henry Williams, a builder and carpenter from Virginia, arrived

in San Francisco in February 1849, when "the town consisted of a few houses about the plaza," and immediately he had more work than he could handle (or hire men for) in constructing frame buildings (Bancroft Collections). By September, he related, prefabricated houses were arriving from the East, and in October he built a brick storehouse three stories high. The gambling saloons may have been the most lavish and usually the first to become permanent structures; this was generally the case, though not without exception. Other statements by Gentry are equally arguable, but as he bases his conclusions on the 1930s account rather than on the original, it is not necessary to include them here.

7. Soulé, Gihon, and Nisbet, *Annals,* p. 668.

8. Ibid., p. 259; Lloyd, *Lights and Shades,* p. 83; Bancroft, *Works,* vol. 23, p. 234.

9. *Alta California,* February 2, 1850; Soulé, Gihon, and Nisbet, *Annals,* p. 355. The Monumental was the first organized firefighting company in the city.

10. *Daily Town Talk,* 1857, ads and announcements of balls.

11. Soulé, Gihon, and Nisbet, *Annals,* pp. 666–68.

12. Ibid. Similar descriptions can be found for different periods throughout the century in Lloyd, *Lights and Shades,* p. 512; Bancroft, *Works,* vol. 24, p. 243; and in the newspapers.

13. *Sunday Varieties,* September 7, 1856. The Prostitutes Ball was apparently a regular event at the Music Hall beginning in 1855; how long it continued is unclear.

14. Such terms are, of course, arbitrary, and it is unlikely that when they were coined it was a prostitute who chose them. They are, however, familiar terms that indicate the "class" of the prostitute—or by my definition, her degree of professionalism. If prostitution was simply viewed as an occupation, they would coincide with such job descriptions as executive, white-collar worker, blue-collar worker, semiskilled laborer, and unskilled laborer.

15. There is no reliable information on a common fee for any category of prostitution. According to Benard de Russailh, *Last Adventure,* and Soulé, Gihon, and Nisbet, *Annals,* a courtesan made from $95 to $400 for one night, depending on whether the year was 1849–1850 or beyond. Apparently the prices graduated downward to a dollar a trick for a dance-hall harlot.

16. Lloyd, *Lights and Shades,* p. 82. See also Janney, M.D., *The White Slave Traffic,* pp. 41–44. In Monterey and Salinas, relics of these structures are preserved and open to the public.

17. Eliza W. Farnham, *California In-Doors and Out,* p. 274; Janney, *White Slave Traffic,* p. 44; Asbury, *Barbary Coast,* p. 260.

18. U.S. census, 1860 and 1870.

19. See *California Police Gazette,* September 14, 1867; Lloyd, *Lights and Shades,* p. 82; see Drago, *Notorious Ladies of the Frontier,* for descriptions of dance halls by name and location.

20. *Municipal Records.* The number of arrests for common prostitution in 1859 were fourteen; 1861, two; and 1863, none. This pattern continued until the 1870s, when a combination of events brought at least a minimal attempt to "prohibit and suppress . . . all houses of ill-fame" and prostitution. The board of supervisors had the power to enforce the prohibition granted to them by the state legislature as early as 1863, but it was not until Chief of Police Cockrill took office in 1874 that there was any significant change in the arrest pattern (one arrest for being an inmate of a house of ill fame in 1862; 89 for the same misdemeanor in 1874). The largest number arrested for soliciting was 547 in 1880, but even that is an insignificant number when it is remembered that there were an estimated three thousand prostitutes working in the Barbary Coast district during this period. Also, the arrests were for misdemeanors, and even when the woman was convicted, only a small fine of $10–$25 was charged, with the woman able to return to her occupation the following day. It is also highly probable that a large percentage of these arrests were against Chinese prostitutes—though the figures are not broken down by ethnic origin—because Chinese women as well as men were victims of anti-Chinese agitation among officials and citizens in San Francisco during the 1870s and 1880s.

21. Carol Wilson, *Gump's Treasure Trade,* p. 34.

22. Ibid., p. 34.

23. Royce, *Frontier Lady,* p. 114.

24. Caleb Fay, Bancroft Dictations, p. 10.

25. Royce, *Frontier Lady,* p. 114.

26. Bancroft, *Works,* vol. 2, p. 240.

27. Ibid., pp. 29, 240.

28. Ibid., p. 31; *Evening Bulletin,* November 21, 1855. Following this incident, James King of William, editor of the *Bulletin,* began one of his periodic campaigns against vice, crime, and municipal corruption in the city.

29. E. D. Baker, *Eloquence of the Far West,* pp. 311–15.

30. William Watkins, Bancroft Collections. Watkins, a member of the 1856 Vigilance Committee, was part of the delegation sent to bring Belle to the place where Charles was confined.

31. Lloyd, *Lights and Shades,* pp. 84–85; Edholm, *Traffic in Girls,* "Seduction and Marriage."

32. Lloyd, *Lights and Shades,* p. 85. It was Lloyd's contention that the working life of a prostitute was four to five months. Since

his goal was to discourage recruitment into the trade, it is safe to assume this is an exaggeration. Nevertheless, all of the factors listed above limited the working years of prostitutes and supports the theory of some writers that the elite sector of the profession moved regularly among the red-light districts of major cities.

33. Bancroft, *Works*, vol. 2, p. 334.

34. U.S. census, 1870.

CHAPTER FOUR. FILLES DE JOIE: THE COSMOPOLITAN ELEMENT

1. Rev. Samuel Willey, Personal Memoirs, Bancroft Manuscripts, pp. 32, 37.

2. Ibid., pp. 74–75.

3. Violence against foreigners could fill a volume of its own. Examples are the "Hounds" attack on Little Chile; the American mob who expelled most of the Latin Americans from Sonora in 1850—including many Californios who were U.S. citizens; the mass violence against the Chinese, ranging from cutting off queues to murder; and the vigilante arrests of Australians thought to be Sydney Ducks. Juanita, a Mexican mistress–prostitute in Downieville, who was hung by a "miners' court" because she had killed a white man who broke into her shack, was the most noted victim of violence against a woman. But beatings and attacks on foreign prostitutes filled newspaper columns devoted to police and recorder courts throughout the rest of the century.

4. Soulé, Gihon, and Nisbet, *Annals*, p. 555; Brown, *Early Days*, pp. 102–05.

5. Soulé, Gihon, and Nisbet, *Annals*, p. 555. The only exception to this typical condemnation was Bancroft, who made a conscious effort to recognize xenophobia and racism and to exclude them from his own works. In *Works*, vol. 25, pp. 233–35, he discusses that the idea of American gold for Americans was used by many forty-niners as an excuse for their violence against non-Americans.

6. Bancroft, *Works*, vol. 1, p. 81.

7. Capitan José Fernandez, Bancroft Collections, pp. 190–91; Soulé, Gihon, and Nisbet, *Annals*, p. 555.

8. Bancroft, *Works*, vol. 23, p. 233.

9. Doten, *Journals*, p. 40.

10. Examples of derogatory references to Latin American prostitutes can be found in the *California Courier*, July 9, 1850; *San Francisco Evening News*, November 4, 1853; *California Police Gazette*, March 20, 1859; Soulé, Gihon, and Nisbet, *Annals*, pp. 412, 472; Isabelle Saxon, *Five Years Within the Golden Gate*, pp. 19–20; and Doten, *Journals*, p. 130. Except for the 1870 census, there are no

lists of prostitutes, as such; but Bancroft refers to French Lenny and Madam Du Bon Court; Doten mentions Doña Isabella; and the newspapers comment on the house of Madam Livingston and other women they designate as courtesans. Although they are not consistent, in some cases they designate the class of the prostitute by terms such as common prostitute, courtesan, madam, and so on.

11. Since Chinese women neither entered the profession nor remained prostitutes by choice, it might be reasonable to question whether they can properly be listed as professionals. The difference in culture, however, must be taken into account. Women in China had virtually no control over their lives. Their father or guardian decided the future for them, and prostitution was merely one of the options. Unlike Western culture, there was no stigma attached to the occupation. For that reason, although they do not fit neatly in my own definition, I have chosen to include Chinese prostitutes among the professionals.

12. Lloyd, *Lights and Shades,* pp. 257–59; Densmore, *Chinese in California,* p. 81; Workingmen's Party, Bancroft Collections, p. 15; Lucie Cheng Hirata, "Free, Indentured, Enslaved."

13. Herbert Asbury, *Barbary Coast,* p. 172; Soulé, Gihon, and Nisbet, *Annals,* p. 384; Carol Berkin and Mary Beth Norton, *Women of America.*

14. Benard de Russailh, *Last Adventure,* p. 88.

15. Most newspapers had daily court columns, and they all carried examples of assaults against prostitutes. See various issues, *San Francisco Evening News,* 1853; *Evening Bulletin,* 1856; and *California Police Gazette,* 1859.

16. Barth, *Bitter Strength,* p. 84, quoting from the *Alta California* regarding Ah Toy; *San Francisco Evening News and Picayune,* November 1, 1855.

17. Workingmen's Party, Bancroft Collections, p. 5.

18. *Municipal Reports,* 1859–1890. City Physician's and Coroner's Reports. These records are yearly summaries and do not break down statistics by race. Occasionally, the official making the report included statements regarding sanitation and health problems in the Chinese areas. However, even the accuracy of these brief statements must be questioned, because they were generally made during periods of active anti-Chinese agitation.

19. Ibid., 1859–60, p. 42.

20. Ibid., 1866–67, p. 132.

21. *California Police Gazette,* January 1866, series of articles and reports on anti-Chinese violence; Yung-Deh Richard Chu, "Chinese Secret Societies."

22. *Municipal Records,* police arrests; U.S. census, 1870.

23. Carol Wilson, *Chinatown Quest,* pp. 12–14, 24.
24. Ibid., p. 17.
25. Bancroft, *Works,* vol. 1, p. 259.
26. Bancroft, *Works,* vol. 23, pp. 222–24. Bancroft writes about the attitudes toward other nationalities and the usefulness of their characteristics in California.
27. *Alta California,* May 24, 1849.
28. Soulé, Gihon, and Nisbet, *Annals,* p. 364; Farnham, *California In-Doors and Out,* p. 272.
29. Soulé, Gihon, and Nisbet, *Annals,* p. 463; *Diary of a Forty-Niner,* p. 6.
30. *Diary of a Forty-Niner,* p. 6.
31. Farnham, *California In-Doors and Out,* p. 272.
32. Benard de Russailh, *Last Adventure,* pp. 27, 29.
33. See Bancroft, *Works,* vol. 2, p. 334, for references to French parlor houses and French residents. See also Benard de Russailh, *Last Adventure,* p. 28. Also see newspapers' arrest columns, such as *California Police Gazette,* March 27, 1859, for comparative references to French and non-French prostitutes.
34. Benard de Russailh, *Last Adventure,* pp. 5–6.
35. Ibid., pp. 16–17, 30. Emphasis mine.
36. Ibid., pp. 18, 23, 26.
37. Soulé, Gihon, and Nisbet, *Annals,* p. 462.

CHAPTER FIVE. WORKING WOMEN

1. Furness, *Genteel Female,* p. 94.
2. Janney, *White Slave Traffic,* p. 40.
3. The U.S. census of 1870 lists numerous married prostitutes whose husbands held a variety of jobs from clerk to saloon owner to brothel keeper.
4. Eliza Farnham, *My Early Days,* p. 394; Helen Holdredge, *Mammy Pleasant's Partner,* pp. 224, 259.
5. Furness, *Genteel Female,* p. 98; as early as 1846, Walt Whitman wrote of the "evils and horrors" brought on by low pay (fifty cents to two dollars a week) for factory women and of the need for reform. Nearly fifty years later, Dorothy Richardson, "The Long Day," related her experience of trying to survive on five dollars a week as a factory girl, in William O'Neill, *Women at Work,* p. 45.
6. *Municipal Records.* Unfortunately, the yearly summaries do not distinguish the number of employees who were women. They simply list, for example: 1869–1870, glove manufacturing, men and women employed, 20; 1885–1886, glove manufacturing, men and women employed, 145.

7. Day, *Hesperian* 1: 216.

8. Ibid. Day's editorial articles usually began with a conciliatory approach apparently aimed at not alienating the readers who would have rejected any hint of a women's-rights stand in the magazine. She might, for example, apologize for writing on subjects more properly thought to belong to the "male sphere" and then go on for two or three columns to condemn the stand other publications—by men—had taken. This method was especially true when she wrote about the position women were given in society.

9. Day, *Hesperian* 1: 61.

10. Lloyd, *Lights and Shades*, p. 247.

11. Soulé, Gihon, and Nisbet, *Annals*, p. 504.

12. Helen Holdredge's biography, *Mammy Pleasant*, demonstrates that women with reputations as superior cooks could command large salaries—$400 a month, at least in 1850. By 1858, when Mrs. Day was publishing the *Hesperian*, conditions had obviously changed, and according to A. W. Morgan and Co.'s *San Francisco City Directory* for 1852, only ten women were listed as running or working in a boarding house. A typical salary was probably closer to the $100 a month earned by a woman hired as cook for a boarding-house/gambling-saloon in Weaverville (Royce, *Frontier Lady*, p. 83).

13. Morgan's *Directory*; Soulé, Gihon, and Nisbet, *Annals*, p. 488.

14. *San Francisco Evening News*, November 1853. The *Daily Town Talk* by 1854—and gradually all newspapers—began carrying cards directed to women customers, including advertisements for ice cream parlors, "the only Fashionable Resort for Ladies and Gentlemen in the State."

15. Helen Campbell, *Prisoners of Poverty*, p. 30.

16. Saxon, *Five Years*, pp. 39–40.

17. Day, *Hesperian* 3:334–35; Saxon, *Five Years*, pp. 24–34.

18. Saxon, *Five Years*, pp. 28–29.

19. Mrs. Charlton Edholm, *Traffic in Girls*, "The Snare of Starvation Wages." Throughout the period there were many social observers and rescue-mission workers—like Edholm—who blamed low pay for women for the spread of prostitution.

20. Soulé, Gihon, Nisbet, *Annals*, p. 503.

21. Royce, *A Frontier Lady*, pp. 109, 114–16.

22. Ibid., pp. 114, 117–19.

23. Bancroft, *Works*, vol. 25, pp. 308–09.

24. Ibid., p. 311.

25. Farnham, *California In-Doors and Out*, pp. 293–94.

26. Ibid., p. 381.

27. Royce's journal *(A Frontier Lady)* of the overland journey in 1849, the hardships, dangers, and fears she faced, and her adaptability to camp living is an amazing account, stoically portrayed, of what it meant to be a pioneer woman.

28. Farnham, *California In-Doors and Out.*

29. Farnham, *Early Days,* p. 394. Farnham did not write the recollections of her youth until after she had published the memoirs of her life in California. Nevertheless, her early experience undoubtedly affected her opinions and writings on the ease with which a woman's reputation could be destroyed.

30. Lloyd, *Lights and Shades,* p. 81; *Sunday Varieties,* June 1, 1856.

31. Lloyd, *Lights and Shades,* pp. 65–66.

32. For a description of the culmination of this concern, which reached almost panic proportions by 1911–1915, see "White Slavery" in Ruth Rosen, *The Lost Sisterhood.*

33. Edholm, *Traffic in Girls,* "How I became a Mission Worker."

34. Ibid., "The Snare of the Mock Marriage and Seduction"; Janney, *White Slave Traffic,* pp. 24–25.

35. Janney, *White Slave Traffic,* pp. 16, 36; Edholm, *Traffic in Girls,* "The Snare of False Employment."

36. Edholm, *Traffic in Girls,* "The Snare of False Employment."

37. Ibid., "The Snare of the Dance"; Janney, *White Slave Traffic,* pp. 83–90.

38. Fictional heroines in the popular periodicals of the period, such as *Godey's Lady's Book,* clearly show the changing attitudes toward the naivete of girls. Fictional heroines of 1848–1849 could easily be seduced, and generally the only fate open to them was death by suicide or decline. By the 1880s, though still innocent and pure, they were more worldly-wise and capable of directing their own actions. Whether the material was meant to be descriptive or prescriptive is difficult to evaluate, but the image makes it even more difficult to accept the passive victim found in white-slave reports.

39. However, there was another view of the reasons for returning. The *California Police Gazette* (October 8, 1857) claimed that San Francisco's House of Refuge was the biggest contributor to "rehabilitated" girls returning to prostitution, since their rehabilitation consisted of scrubbing floors and doing other menial tasks.

40. Serge Wolsey, *Call House Madam,* and Erwin and Miller, *Orderly Disorderly House,* describe two madams' entrance into the profession and the experiences of the prostitutes who worked for them. Janney, *White Slave Traffic,* pp. 21–22, allows the existence of "victims" who stayed in prostitution because of money

and excitement, but these were, in his reports, foreign girls, not American.

41. Woolston, *Prostitution in the United States,* pp. 159–78.

42. The controversy over the extent of the white-slave traffic in America can be found in numerous contemporary sources, such as Janney, *White Slave Traffic,* Edholm, *Traffic in Girls,* Addams, *New Conscience,* and Woolston, *Prostitution in the United States,* as well as in modern sources, such as Rosen, *The Lost Sisterhood,* Connelly, *Response to Prostitution,* and Bullough and Bullough, *Prostitution.*

43. *Municipal Records,* coroner's reports.

CHAPTER SIX. ON THE FRINGE: CORRUPTION AND REFORM

1. Soulé, Gihon, and Nisbet, *Annals,* p. 212; Bancroft, *Works,* vol. 25, p. 234.

2. Lloyd, *Lights and Shades,* p. 83; Soulé, Gihon, and Nisbet, *Annals,* p. 463. According to the 1860 U.S. census, there were 497 mantua makers and 214 milliners in all of California. The female population at that time was approximately 107 thousand. Generally it is assumed that both occupations are held by women, but as seen in chapter 4, this assumption cannot be made for San Francisco or California. Since both occupations refer to designers and not to those who actually sewed the fashions, it is not possible to list these occupations (as one can more confidently do with the 492 seamstresses in California), as being filled by women. It is reasonable to assume, however, that some were women and that both men and women employed in these "respectable" occupations were able to profit financially because of prostitution.

3. Lloyd, *Lights and Shades,* p. 66.

4. Soulé, Gihon, and Nisbet, *Annals,* p. 464.

5. Ibid., p. 83.

6. Lloyd, *Lights and Shades,* p. 446.

7. Ibid.; Clappe, *Shirley Letters,* p. 3.

8. Soulé, Gihon, and Nisbet, *Annals,* p. 370.

9. Henriques, *Prostitution and Society,* vol. 2, p. 148.

10. Lloyd, *Lights and Shades,* p. 146.

11. Claudia Johnson, "Guilty Third Tier," p. 580.

12. Ibid., p. 577; Lloyd, *Lights and Shades,* p. 154.

13. Johnson, "Guilty Third Tier," p. 577; Lloyd, *Lights and Shades,* p. 157; Soulé, Gihon, and Nisbet, *Annals,* p. 655.

14. Fremont Older, *My Own Story,* pp. 101–03; Walton Bean, *Boss Ruef's San Francisco,* pp. 50–51. The houses of prostitution in this case were called French restaurants. A respectable family res-

taurant occupied the ground floor, private dining rooms occupied the second floor, and the floors above were dining–bedrooms used by prostitutes or as rooms of assignation. Reports of similar collusion can be found in articles on other western towns: see Carol Leonard and Isidor Wallimann, "Prostitution and Changing Morality in Frontier Cattle Towns of Kansas"; Marion Goldman, "Sexual Commerce on the Comstock Lode"; and Joel Best, "Keeping the Peace in St. Paul."

15. Charles Howe, Bancroft Dictations.

16. Bancroft, *Works,* vol. 25, p. 605.

17. Bancroft, *Works,* vol. 2, pp. 249, 264, 334.

18. Lloyd, *Lights and Shades,* p. 412; Farnham, *California In-Doors and Out,* p. 94.

19. *Lights and Shades,* p. 256. In this instance, Lloyd is referring to police working in the Chinese quarter, but he makes similar references to police in the Barbary Coast and in the city and county prisons.

20. Acton, *Prostitution,* p. 208; Lloyd, *Lights and Shades,* p. 83.

21. Soulé, Gihon, and Nisbet, *Annals,* p. 498; Brown, *Early Days,* pp. 88–89, includes the prices of rent to individual gamblers for a table ($200 per day) if they could not afford to buy or rent a building.

22. Franklin Hichborn, Bancroft Collections, 1908 report, pp. 5–6; Farnham, *California In-Doors and Out,* p. 273.

23. See *Sunday Varieties,* June 1, 1856; and *California Police Gazette,* August 27, 1859; June 30, 1860; October 28, 1865; and September 14, 1867.

24. *California Police Gazette,* March 20, 1859.

25. Janney, *White Slave Traffic,* p. 28.

26. Edholm, *Traffic in Girls,* "The Snare of Mock Marriage and Seduction."

27. See Wilson, *Chinatown Quest,* p. 12; Janney, *White Slave Traffic,* p. 32. Lloyd, *Lights and Shades,* p. 260, sets the price at $600 for Chinese prostitutes in the 1870s. Bancroft, *Works,* vol. 25, p. 563, puts the price at $400 in the 1850s and 1860s.

28. Newspaper and journal accounts seldom suggest that cadets were connected with more than one prostitute at a time.

29. See Erwin and Miller, *Orderly Disorderly House,* pp. 203–04; Davis, *American Heroine,* p. 114; Edholm, *Traffic in Girls,* "Mock Marriage"; Janney, *White Slave Traffic,* p. 35, on the role of pimp in the nineteenth or twentieth century. None are conclusive; none contain first-hand accounts by pimps. Like these writers, I have drawn my own conclusions from the statements made by others.

30. Lloyd, *Lights and Shades,* p. 337.

31. *California Police Gazette,* October 8, 1859.

32. Dobie, *San Francisco's Chinatown,* p. 234.

33. Edholm, *Traffic in Girls,* "How I Became a Mission Worker."

34. Cunnington, *Feminine Attitudes,* p. 92. Smith-Rosenberg ("Beauty, the Beast, and the Militant Woman") discusses the activities of women attempting to close the brothels and end the double standard in the 1830s.

CHAPTER SEVEN. SAN FRANCISCO SOCIETY: THE VICTORIAN INFLUENCE

1. Benard de Russailh, *Last Adventure,* p. 30.
2. Bancroft, *Works,* vol. 25, p. 317.
3. *Municipal Records,* chief of police report, 1860. See Henriques, *Prostitution and Society,* p. 24, on the development of the double standard.
4. Acton, *Prostitution,* p. 198.
5. Ibid., pp. 198, 202–03.
6. See *Alta California,* February 5, 1850; Benard de Russailh, *Last Adventure,* p. 27.
7. Soulé, Gihon, and Nisbet, *Annals,* pp. 259, 364; Bancroft, *Works,* vol. 25, p. 309.
8. Crosby, Bancroft Collections, p. 126.
9. Ibid.
10. Reverend A. H. Tevis, *Beyond the Sierras,* p. 118; also see Bancroft, *Works,* vol. 25, p. 258.
11. Tevis, *Beyond the Sierras,* p. 26.
12. Ibid., p. 18.
13. Commentary on just about every aspect of the immigrants' life in California, including the reasons for coming, staying, and leaving, can be found in the gold-rush songs. See: Eleanora Black, *The Gold Rush Song Book;* Kiley Mains, "The Good Old Days of '50 and '1 and '2," Bancroft Collections; and Richard Dwyer and Richard Lingenfelter, *Songs of the Gold Rush.*
14. James Riordan, Letters 1859–1861, Bancroft Collections. Many diaries and journals of the period reveal the doggedness of the miners in their search for the elusive bonanza strike, but Riordan's letters to his brother and sister illustrate the confidence that was maintained despite failure after failure.
15. Soulé, Gihon, and Nisbet, *Annals,* p. 130. Attitudes toward prostitution and changing values are covered in other works not dealing with San Francisco: William Howard Moore, "Pietism and Progress"; Carol Leonard, "Prostitution and Changing Social Norms"; Vern Bullough, "Women, Birth Control, Prostitution and the Pox"; David Pivar, *Purity Crusade.*
16. Lloyd, *Lights and Shades,* p. 469.

17. Even on the trail to California, the wagons with women in them were easily spotted because the campsites looked like parlors or kitchens with log perimeters and chairs or bedding sectioning off the "rooms" (Royce, *A Frontier Lady,* pp. 3–24). Royce is very detailed in her descriptions of each new locale and of her attempts to make the family tent or shack or a San Francisco boarding house resemble home.

18. Lloyd, *Lights and Shades,* p. 108; Tevis, *Beyond the Sierras,* p. 129.

19. U.S. census, 1860. More than forty foreign countries were represented in California.

20. Because of the limitations of the 1860 census reports, these percentages are approximate, taken from the aggregate totals of individual states in the 1860 census, and refer to all of California rather than San Francisco exclusively. Also it should be remembered that the 35 percent native-born Californians included Indians, Mexican-Californios, and probably many of the approximately sixty thousand children under ten years of age present in the state. The immigrants, on the other hand, were primarily adult white males with full citizenship rights; by 1860, the number also included many of the immigrants' wives.

21. Farnham, *California In-Doors and Out,* pp. 264–65.

22. Lloyd, *Lights and Shades,* p. 511.

23. Ibid., p. 80.

24. Soulé, Gihon, and Nisbet, *Annals,* p. 362.

25. Ibid., p. 503.

26. Edward Howe, Bancroft Collections. This sentiment can be frequently found in the diaries and letters of the immigrants.

27. Soulé, Gihon, and Nisbet, *Annals,* pp. 502–03.

28. Benard de Russailh, *Last Adventure,* p. 15, having observed brawls and fights where no one interfered with the combatants, wondered "if these great people will revert altogether to barbarism."

29. *California Police Gazette,* July 1, 1867.

30. Ibid., February 27, 1859.

31. Farnham, *California In-Doors and Out,* pp. 298–99.

32. *Hesperian,* 1858, pp. 15, 26, 56; 1860, p. 45.

33. Farnham, *California In-Doors and Out,* pp. 302–03. Furness, *Genteel Female,* pp. 194–200, quotes many of the passages from Farnham's views on women in California; *Hesperian,* 1858, pp. 32, 58, made similar observations.

34. Lloyd, *Lights and Shades,* pp. 449, 466. An interesting contrast to this life-style can be found in Peter Gay "Discreet Pleasures."

35. Lloyd, *Lights and Shades,* pp. 380–84; White, *Yankee Trader,*

p. 176; Royce, *Frontier Lady,* pp. 116–17; Frederick Macondray, Bancroft Collections; and Saxon, *Five Years,* p. 55 all note with alarm the rising divorce rate in San Francisco. In 1875 there were 600 applicants for divorce; there were four female applicants to every one male applicant.

36. Lloyd, *Lights and Shades,* p. 384.
37. Sallie Snow, Bancroft Collections.
38. Saxon, *Five Years,* pp. 58–59.
39. Ibid., p. 25.
40. Oscar Lewis, *The Big Four,* pp. 97–98.
41. Ibid., pp. 87, 100, 129, and 197, describes the display of wealth and "culture" as practiced by the big four and their wives.
42. Eleanor Flexner, *Century of Struggle,* pp. 209–12; Sophonisba P. Breckinridge, *Women in the Twentieth Century,* pp. 3–4. Cameron's Settlement House, Edholm's Rescue Mission, and Addams's Hull House were all started in the 1880s.
43. Smith, *Daughters of the Promised Land,* pp. 67, 163–74. See also Edholm, *Traffic in Girls,* Addams, *New Conscience,* Wilson, *Chinatown Quest,* and Hichborn, Bancroft Collections.
44. Carroll Smith-Rosenberg, "Beauty, the Beast and the Militant Woman." In stating that agitation against the double standard lessened during the high point of Victorian culture (1850–1870), I do not intend to ignore the publications and speeches of women's-rights advocates that argued for total equality, for a relaxation of divorce laws, and for a woman's right to control of her own body. These writings and speeches, however, were seldom part of the typically Victorian literature. In *Godey's* and other magazines and journals of this type, such as *Ladies' Wreath, Waverly,* and *Ladies' Companion,* moral messages were conveyed prescriptively and were changed throughout the period. In 1845, a typical story included a seduced heroine who was shunned by society and a man who was accepted until his improper behavior was exposed. In 1860, such men seldom made their appearance except as complete villains who fooled only the shallow members of society. By the 1880s, the double standard was again evident, although the heroine was seldom seduced, being discerning enough to see the immoral man for what he was even if he was able to fool society for a time.
45. *Bulletin,* January 21, 22, 24, 1856.
46. *Hesperian,* 1858, p. 72.
47. Ibid., p. 120.
48. Ibid., p. 104.
49. Bancroft Collections.
50. Lloyd, *Lights and Shades,* p. 83.
51. Edholm, *Traffic in Girls,* "Seduction and Marriage."

CHAPTER EIGHT. EPILOGUE

1. One prostitute in the 1850s regretted only "that she had not double capacity for increasing her gains" (Garniss, Bancroft Collections). My own interviews with three prostitutes in Santa Cruz, San Francisco, and Berkeley, in May, October, and December 1975, in January 1976, and a follow-up interview in Santa Cruz in 1980, bear this out. These women discussed their motivations, their experiences, and their reactions to my own conclusions.

2. Interviews in note 1.

3. Wolsey, *Call House Madam*, p. 231.

4. Garniss, Bancroft Collections, p. 22.

5. Stanford, *Lady of the House*, p. 71. In the interviews mentioned in note 1, prostitutes gave similar opinions of subconscious-motive explanations.

6. Stanford, *Lady of the House*, pp. 10–11.

7. Ibid., pp. 68–69. Stanford relates the incident of Smith in her own inimitable style, but accounts of his activities were fully covered in the newspapers.

8. Ibid., pp. 45–47.

9. *Newsweek*, July 8, 1974, p. 65; *San Francisco Magazine* 17:26; *San Francisco Chronicle*, March 11, 1976.

10. *San Francisco Chronicle*, May 10, 1975.

11. August 23, 1983.

12. *San Francisco Magazine* 16: 14, 18.

13. Soulé, Gihon, and Nisbet, *Annals*, p. 550.

14. *San Francisco Magazine* 16: 14.

BIBLIOGRAPHY

BOOKS

Acton, William. *Prostitution.* 1857. Reprint. New York: Frederick A. Praeger, 1968.

Addams, Jane. *A New Conscience and an Ancient Evil.* New York: Macmillan, 1912.

Adler, Polly. *A House Is Not a Home.* New York: Rinehart, 1953.

Asbury, Herbert. *The Barbary Coast.* Long Beach, Calif.: Brown and Nourse, 1949.

———. *The French Quarter.* New York: Knopf, 1936.

Baker, E. D. *Eloquence of the Far West.* Edited by Oscar T. Shuck. San Francisco: 1899.

Bancroft, Caroline. *Six Racy Madams of Colorado.* Johnson Books, 1965.

Bancroft, Hubert Howe. *The Works of Hubert Howe Bancroft.* 39 vols. San Francisco: History Co., 1886–1888.

Banner, Lois. *Women in Modern America.* New York: Harcourt Brace Jovanovich, 1974.

Barth, Gunther. *Bitter Strength: A History of the Chinese in the United States, 1850–1870.* Cambridge: Harvard University Press, 1964.

Bean, Walton. *Boss Reuf's San Francisco.* Berkeley: University of California Press, 1972.

———. *California: An Interpretive History.* New York: McGraw-Hill, 1968.

Beans, Rowena. *"Inasmuch . . ."; The One Hundred-Year History of the San Francisco Ladies' Protection and Relief Society.* San Francisco: 1953.

Benard de Russailh, Albert. *Last Adventure.* Translated by Clarkson Crane. San Francisco: Westgate, 1931.

Berkin, Carol R., Norton, Mary Beth, eds. *Women of America: A History.* Boston: Houghton Mifflin, 1979.

Black, Eleanora. *The Gold Rush Song Book.* San Francisco: Colt, 1940.

Breckinridge, Sophonisba P. *Women in the Twentieth Century.* New York: McGraw-Hill, 1933.

Brown, Dee. *The Gentle Tamers.* New York: Bantam, 1974.

Brown, John Henry. *Early Days of San Francisco, California.* 1886. Reprint. Oakland: Biobooks, 1949.

Buchannan, A. Russell. *David S. Terry of California: Dueling Judge.* San Marino: Huntington Library, 1956.

Bullough, Vern, and Bullough, Bonnie. *Prostitution: An Illustrated Social History.* New York: Crown, 1978.

———. *A Bibliography of Prostitution.* New York: Garland, 1977.

Campbell, Helen. *Prisoners of Poverty.* Westport, Conn.: Greenwood Press, 1970.

Castelot, André. *Josephine.* Translated by Denise Folliot. New York: Harper and Row, 1967.

Chandra, Moti. *World of Courtesans.* New York: International Book Distributors, 1974.

Clappe, Louise A. K. S. (Dame Shirley). *The Shirley Letters.* Santa Barbara: Peregrine Smith, 1970. (First published in *Pioneer Magazine,* 1854 and 1855.)

Cohn, David. *The Good Old Days: A History of American Morals and Manners as Seen Through the Sears, Roebuck Catalogs, 1905 to the Present.* New York: Simon and Schuster, 1940.

Connelly, Mark T. *The Response to Prostitution in the Progressive Era.* Chapel Hill: University of North Carolina Press, 1980.

Cunnington, C. Willett. *Feminine Attitudes in the Nineteenth Century.* New York: Macmillan, 1936.

Davis, Allen. *American Heroine: The Life and Legend of Jane Addams.* Boston: Oxford University Press, 1973.

Decker, John. *Prostitution: Regulation and Control.* Littleton, Colo.: Rothman, 1979.

Densmore, G. B. *The Chinese in California: Descriptions of Chinese Life in San Francisco, their Habits, Morals, and Manners.* San Francisco: Pettit and Russ, 1880.

Derbec, Etienne. *A French Journalist in the California Gold Rush: The Letters of Etienne Derbec.* Edited by A. P. Nasatir. Georgetown, Calif.: Talisman, 1964.

DeWulf, Lucienne. *Faces of Venus: Prostitution Through the Ages.* Books in Focus, forthcoming.

Diary of a Forty-Niner. 1881. Reprint. Edited by Chauncey L. Canfield. Stanford: James Ladd Delkin, 1947.

Dobie, Charles Caldwell. *San Francisco's Chinatown.* New York: Appleton-Century, 1936.

Dock, Lavina. *Hygiene and Morality: Manual for Nurses.* New York: Putnam and Sons, 1910.

Doten, Alfred. *The Journals of Alfred Doten, 1849–1903.* 3 vols. Edited by Walter Van Tilburg Clark. Reno: University of Nevada Press, 1973.

Doxey's Guide to San Francisco and Vicinity. San Francisco: Doxey, 1881.

Drago, H. S. *Notorious Ladies of the Frontier.* New York: Dodd, Mead, 1969.

Dunn, Allan. *Care-Free San Francisco.* San Francisco: A. M. Robertson, 1912.

Dwyer, Richard A., and Lingenfelter, Richard E., eds. *The Songs of the Gold Rush.* Berkeley: University of California Press, 1964.

Edholm, Mrs. Charlton (Mary Grace). *Traffic in Girls and Work of the Rescue Mission.* Oakland: Mrs. Charlton Edholm, 1900.

Engel, *Brothels of Nevada.* Los Angeles, Calif.: Holloway, 1980.

Erwin, Carol, with Miller, Floyd. *The Orderly Disorderly House.* New York: Doubleday, 1960.

Evans, Hilary. *Harlots, Whores, and Hookers.* New York: Taplinger, 1979.

Farnham, Eliza W. *California In-Doors and Out; or How We Farm, Mine and Live Generally in the Golden State.* New York: Dix, Edwards, 1856.

———. *My Early Days.* New York: Thatcher and Hutchinson, 1859.

Finnegan, Frances. *Poverty and Prostitution: A Study of Victorian Prostitutes in New York.* New York: Cambridge University Press, 1979.

Flexner, Eleanor, *Century of Struggle.* New York: Atheneum, 1971.

Foley, Doris. *Lola Montez: The Divine Eccentric.* New York: Ballantine, 1969.

Fowler, William. *Women of the American Frontier.* Hartford, Conn.: S. S. Seranton, 1878.

Frazer, James George. *The New Golden Bough.* New York: Criterion, 1959.

Friedman, Jean, and Slade, William, eds. *Our American Sisters.* Boston: Allyn and Bacon, 1973.

Furness, Clifton J. *The Genteel Female.* New York: Knopf, 1931.

Gay, Peter. *Education of the Senses: Victoria to Freud.* New York: Oxford University Press, 1984.

Geertz, Clifford. *An Interpretation of Cultures.* New York: Basic, 1973.

Gentry, Curt. *The Madams of San Francisco: A Highly Irreverent History.* New York: Signet, 1964.

Goldman, Emma. *The Traffic in Women and Other Essays on Feminism.* New York: Times Change, 1971.

Goldman, Marion S. *Gold Diggers and Silver Miners: Prostitution and Social Life on the Comstock Lode.* Ann Arbor: University of Michigan Press, 1981.

Gordon, Michael, ed. *The American Family in Social-History Perspective.* New York: St. Martin's, 1973.

Hadden, Maude. *The Slavery of Prostitution: a plea for emancipation.* New York: Macmillan, 1916.

Hall, Geoffrey Fowler. *Moths Round the Flame: Studies of Charmers and Intriguers.* Freeport, N.Y.: Books for Libraries, 1969.

Harris, Henry. *Human Merchandise.* London: E. Bern, 1928.

Helper, Hinton. *Dredful California.* Edited by Lucius Beebe and Charles M. Clegg. New York: Bobbs-Merrill, 1948.

Henriques, Fernando. *Prostitution and Society.* 3 vols. London: MacGibbon and Kee, 1965–1968.

Heyl, Barbara. *The Madam as Entrepreneur: Career Management in House Prostitution.* New Brunswick, N.J.: Transaction, 1978.

Holdredge, Helen. *Mammy Pleasant.* New York: G. P. Putnam's Sons, 1950.

———. *Mammy Pleasant's Partner.* New York: G. P. Putnam's Sons, 1954.

Horn, Pierre L., and Pringle, Mary B. *The Image of the Prostitute in Modern Literature.* New York: Ungar, 1984.

Hunt, Harriet K. *Glimpses and Glances: or Fifty Years Social Including Twenty Years Professional Life.* Boston: John P. Jewett, 1856.

Hutson, Jon. *The Chicken Ranch.* Scarsdale, N.Y.: S. Barnes, 1980.

Jacobson, Pauline. *City of the Golden 'Fifties.* Berkeley: University of California Press, 1941.

Janney, O. Edward. *The White Slave Traffic in America.* New York: National Vigilance Committee, 1911.

Jones, Idwal. *Ark of Empire: San Francisco's Unique Bohemia, 1853–1953.* New York: Ballantine, 1972.

Kraditor, Aileen, ed. *Up From the Pedestal.* Chicago: Quadrangle, 1968.

Lasagna, Louis. *The V.D. Epidemic.* Philadelphia: Temple University Press, 1975.

Lee, C. Y. *Days of the Tong Wars.* New York: Ballantine, 1974.

Lewis, Oscar. *Bay Window Bohemia.* New York: Doubleday, 1956.

———. *The Big Four.* New York: Ballantine, 1971.

———. *San Francisco: Mission to Metropolis.* Berkeley: Howell-North, 1966.

Lloyd, Benjamin E. *Lights and Shades in San Francisco.* San Francisco: A. L. Bancroft, 1876.

Long, Mason. *Save the Girls.* Fort Wayne: M. Long, 1888.

McDonald, Douglas. *Julia Bulette and the Red Light Ladies of Nevada.* Reno: Nevada Publications, 1980.

McHugh, Paul. *Prostitution and Victorian Social Reform.* New York: St. Martin's, 1980.

Marcus, Steven. *The Other Victorians: A Study of Sexuality and*

Pornography in Mid-Nineteenth Century England. New York: Basic, 1964.

Martin, Cy. *Whiskey and Wild Women.* New York: Hart, 1974.

Milford, Nancy. *Madame De Pompadore.* New York: Harper and Row, 1954.

Miller, Ronald. *Shady Ladies of the West.* Los Angeles: Westernland, 1964.

New York Committee of Fifteen 1900. *The Social Evil.* New York: G. P. Putnam's Sons, 1902.

O'Callaghan, Sean. *The White Slave.* London, 1965.

Older, Fremont. *My Own Story.* New York: Macmillan, 1926.

O'Neil, William, ed. *Women at Work.* Chicago: Quadrangle, 1972.

Paul, Rodman W. *California Gold.* Lincoln: University of Nebraska Press, 1949.

Pearson, Michael. *The Age of Consent: Victorian Prostitution and Its Enemies.* Newton Abbot, 1972.

Pivar, David. *Purity Crusade: Sexual Morality and Social Control, 1868–1900.* Westport: Greenwood, 1973.

Pomeroy, Sarah. *Goddesses, Whores, Wives, and Slaves: Women in Classical Antiquity.* New York: Schocken, 1975.

Prostitution in the Victorian Age: Debates on the Issue From Nineteenth Century Critical Journals. London: Gregg International, 1973.

Riencourt, Amaury de. *Sex and Power in History.* New York: Dell, 1974.

Robinson, D. G. *Comic Songs: or, Hits at San Francisco.* San Francisco Commercial, 1853.

Rose, Al. *Storyville, New Orleans.* Tuscaloosa: University of Alabama Press, 1974.

Rosen, Ruth. *The Lost Sisterhood: Prostitution in America 1900–1918.* Baltimore: Johns Hopkins University Press, 1982.

Rosen, Ruth, and Davidson, Sue, eds. *The Mamie Papers.* Old Westbury, NY: Feminist, 1977.

Royce, Josiah. *California From the Conquest in 1846 to the Second Vigilance Committee in San Francisco.* Santa Barbara: Peregrine Smith, 1970.

Royce, Sarah. *A Frontier Lady.* Edited by Ralph Henry Gabriel. New Haven: Yale University Press, 1932.

Ryan, Mary P. *Womanhood in America From Colonial Times to the Present.* New York: New Viewpoints, 1975.

Sanger, William W. *The History of Prostitution: Its Extent, Causes, and Effects Throughout the World.* 1857. Reprint. New York: Eugenics, 1937.

Saxon, Isabelle. *Five Years Within the Golden Gate.* London: Chapman and Hall, 1868.

Seibert, Ilse. *Women in the Ancient Near East.* Translated by Marianne Herzfeld. New York: Abner Schram, 1974.

Sion, Abraham. *Prostitution and the Law.* Winchester, Mass.: Faber and Faber, 1978.

Smith, Page. *Daughters of the Promised Land.* Boston: Little, Brown, 1970.

Soulé, Frank; Gihon, John H.; and Nisbet, James. *The Annals of San Francisco.* 1855. Reprint. Compiled by Dorothy H. Huggins. Palo Alto: Lewis Osborne, 1966.

Stanford, Sally. *The Lady of the House.* New York: Putnam, 1966.

Stewart, Elinore Pruitt. *Letters of a Woman Homesteader.* Lincoln, Neb.: Bison, 1961.

Taylor, William. *Seven Years' Street Preaching in San Francisco, California.* New York: Carlton and Porter, 1856.

Tevis, A. H. *Beyond the Sierras.* Philadelphia: J. B. Lippincott, 1877.

Thornwell, Emily. *The Complete Guide to Gentility.* Reprint of 1856 edition. San Marino, Calif.: The Huntington Library, 1979.

Vilas, Martin. *The Barbary Coast of San Francisco.* Burlington: Vermont Free Press, 1915.

Vogliotti, Gabriel R. *The Girls of Nevada.* New Jersey: Citadel, 1975.

Walkowitz, Judith. *Prostitution and Victorian Society: Women, Class, and the State.* New York: Cambridge University Press, 1980.

Wecter, Dixon. *The Saga of American Society: A Record of Social Aspiration 1607–1937.* New York: Charles Scribner's Sons, 1937.

West, Elliot, and Martin, Cy. *Whiskey and Wild Women: An Amusing Account of the Saloons and Bawds of the Old West.* New York: Hart, 1974.

White, Katherine, ed. *A Yankee Trader in the Gold Rush: The Letters of Franklin H. Buck.* Boston: Houghton Mifflin, 1930.

Williams, George J., III. *The Redlight Ladies of Virginia City, Nevada.* Riverside, Calif.: Tree by River, 1984.

Wilson, Carol Green. *Chinatown Quest: The Life Adventures of Donaldina Cameron.* Stanford: Stanford University Press, 1931.

———. *Gump's Treasure Trade.* New York: Crowell, 1949.

Wilson, Jackson. *The Harlots and the Pharisees.* Berkeley: University of California Press, 1913.

Winick, Charles. *The Lively Commerce.* Chicago: Quadrangle, 1971.

Wolsey, Serge G. *Call House Madam: the Story of the Career of Beverly Davis.* San Francisco: Martin Tudordale, 1943.

Woolston, Howard. *Prostitution in the United States Prior to the Entrance of the United States into the World War.* 1921. Reprint. Montclair, N.J.: Patterson Smith, 1969.

JOURNALS, PAMPHLETS, PUBLIC RECORDS, MAGAZINES, AND DISSERTATIONS

Allaman, John Lee. "The Crime, Trial, and Execution of William W. Lee of East Burlington, Illinois." *Western Illinois Regional Studies* 6 (1983): 49–66.

Auerbach, Alvin. "San Francisco's South of Market District, 1850–1950: The Emergence of a Skid Row." *California Historical Quarterly* 52 (1973): 192–223.

Best, Joel. "Keeping the Peace in St. Paul: Crime, Vice, and Police Work, 1869–1874." *Minnesota History* 47 (1981): 240–48.

Blackburn, George, and Ricards, Sherman L. "The Chinese of Virginia City, Nevada: 1870." *Amerasia* 7 (1980): 51–72.

———. "The Prostitutes and Gamblers of Virginia City, Nevada: 1870." *Pacific Historical Review* 48 (1979): 239–58.

Bullough, Vern. "Women: Birth Control, Prostitution and the Pox." *Social and Administrative History* 6 (1976): 20–28.

Butler, Anne Katherine. "The Tarnished Frontier: Prostitution in the Trans-Mississippi West, 1865–1890." Ph.D. dissertation, University of Maryland, 1979.

Butler, Anne M. "Military Myopia: Prostitution on the Frontier." *Prologue* 13 (1981): 233–50.

Chu, Yung-Deh Richard. "Chinese Secret Societies in America: A Historical Survey." *Asian Profile* (Hong Kong) 1 (1973): 21–38.

"Constitution and By-Laws of the San Francisco 'Ladies' Protection and Relief Society.'" 1853. *Pamphlets on San Francisco.*

Day, Mrs. F. H. *The Hesperian.* (Ladies literary journal published 1858 through 1861.)

Davis, W. N. "Research Uses of County Court Records, 1850–1879: and Incidental Intimate Glimpses of California Life and Society, Part I." *California Historical Quarterly* 52 (1973): 241–66.

Degler, Carl N. "Women's Sexuality in the Nineteenth Century." *The American Historical Review* 79 (1974): 1467–90.

de Graaf, Lawrence B. "Race, Sex, and Region: Black Women in the American West." *Pacific Historical Review* 49 (1980): 285–313.

Garrison, Dee. "Immoral Fiction in the Late Victorian Library." *American Quarterly* 28 (1976): 71–89.

Gay, Peter. "The Discreet Pleasures of the Bourgeoisie." *The American Scholar* (Winter 1983–1984): 91–99.

Godey's (Magazine and) Lady's Book. Philadelphia, 1845–1895.

Goldman, Marion. "Sexual Commerce on the Comstock Lode." *Nevada Historical Society Quarterly* 21 (1978): 98–129.

Graff, Harvey. " 'Pauperism, Misery, and Vice': Illiteracy and Criminality in the Nineteenth Century." *Journal of Social History* 11 (1977): 245–68.

Hirata, Lucie Cheng. "Free, Indentured, Enslaved: Chinese Prostitutes in Nineteenth Century America." *Signs* 5 (1979): 3–29.

Howe, Daniel W. "American Victorianism as a Culture." *American Quarterly* 27 (1975): 507–32.

Ichioka, Yuji. "Ameyuki-San: Japanese Prostitutes in Nineteenth-Century America." *Amerasia* 4 (1977): 1–21.

Johnson, Claudia D. "That Guilty Third Tier: Prostitution in Nineteenth-Century American Theaters." *American Quarterly* 27 (1975): 575–85.

Leonard, Carol, and Wallimann, Isidor. "Prostitution and Changing Morality in the Frontier Cattle Towns of Kansas." *Kansas History* 2 (1979): 34–53.

Leonard, Carol. "Prostitution and Changing Social Norms in America." Ph.D. diss., Syracuse University, 1979.

Lubove, Ray. "The Progressive and the Prostitute." *The Historian* 24 (1962): 208–330.

Moore, William Howard. "Pietism and Progress: James H. Hayford and the Wyoming Anti-Gambling Tradition, 1869–1893." *Annals of Wyoming* 55 (1983): 2–8.

Municipal Records of San Francisco: Reports to the Board of Supervisors. 31 vols. 1859–1890.

Petrik, Paula. "Capitalists With Rooms: Prostitution in Helena, Montana, 1865–1900." *Montana* 31 (1981): 28–41.

Riegal, Robert E. "Changing American Attitudes Toward Prostitution (1800–1920)." *The Journal of the History of Ideas* 29 (1968): 437–52.

Rosenburg, Charles E. "Sexuality, Class and Role in Nineteenth Century America." *American Quarterly* 25 (1973): 132–53.

Smith, Mary Roberts. "Almshouse Women." *Quarterly Publications of the American Statistical Association* (September 1895).

Smith-Rosenburg, Carroll. "Beauty, the Beast, and the Militant Woman." *American Quarterly* 23 (1971): 562–84.

Symanski, Richard. "Prostitution in Nevada." *Annals of the Association of American Geographers* 64 (1974): 357–77.

Tansey, Richard. "Prostitution and Politics in Antebellum New Orleans." *Southern Studies* 18 (1979): 449–79.

Walkowitz, Judith, and Walkowitz, Daniel. " 'We Are Not Beasts of the Field': Prostitution and the Poor in Plymouth and Southampton Under the Contagious Diseases Acts." *Feminist's Studies* 1 (1973): 73–106.

West, Elliott. "Scarlet West: The Oldest Profession in the Trans-Mississippi West." *Montana* 31 (1981): 16–27.

Wood, Ann D. "The 'Scribbling Women' and Fanny Fern: Why Women Wrote." *American Quarterly* 23 (1971): 3–24.

Wunsch, James. "The Social Evil Ordinance." *American Heritage* 33 (1982): 50–55.

BANCROFT MANUSCRIPT COLLECTIONS, BERKELEY, CALIFORNIA

Appleton, E. "Bella Union Melodeon Songster." 1860.

Clemens, Max Richter. Autobiography and Reminiscences. 1872.

Coon, Henry Perrin. "Annals of San Francisco." C. 1878.

Crosby, Elisha Oscar. "Events in California." C. 1878.

Dows, James. "Statement on Vigilance Committee in San Francisco." 1877.

Fay, Caleb T. "Statement of Historical Facts on California." 1878.

Fernandez, Capitan José. "*Cosas de California.*" 1874.

Fernandez, Don Juan. *Colección de Documentos para la Historia de California.* 1840–1850. 1874.

Garniss, James R. "The Early Days of San Francisco." 1877.

Hays, Benjamin. *Scraps.* Vol. 60. 1850–1900.

Hichborn, Franklin. "The Social Evil in California as a Political Problem." C. 1914.

Howe, Charles. Reminiscences of 1849. C. 1873.

Howe, Edward Robbins. Letters and Papers. 1869–1873.

Larkin, Thomas. Miscellaneous Statements on California. C. 1870.

Macondray, Frederick W. Letters. C. 1859.

Mains, J. Kiley. "The Good Old Days of '50 and '1 and '2. Answer to the 'Days of '49' " (song). C. 1853.

Riordan, James. Letters. 1859–1861.

Snow, Sallie. Letters. 1868.

Stevens, Harriet. "The American Woman as a Frontier in Modern Civilization." 1892.

Watkins, William. "Statement on Vigilance Committee." 1878.

Willey, Samuel. Personal Memoirs. C. 1870.

Williams, Henry. "Statement of Recollections on Early Days of California." 1878.

Workingmen's Party of California. "Chinatown Declared a Nuisance!" 1870.

NEWSPAPERS

Alta California
California Courier
Californian
California Police Gazette
California Star
Daily Town Talk
Evening Bulletin
Oakland Tribune
The Phoenix (Ubiquitous)
San Francisco Call
San Francisco Chronicle
San Francisco Daily Herald
San Francisco Evening News and Picayune
San Francisco Examiner
San Francisco News Letter
Santa Cruz Sentinel
Shop and Senate
The Sun
Sunday Varieties
The WASP
The Workingmen's Journal

INDEX